44

84

MW01115187

Welcome!

While every quilt is a work of art, it's the comfort a quilt can bring both physically and emotionally that draws me to this craft. Making a quilt is truly a labor of love. It carries the story of the person who carefully crafted it, as well as memories of those who use it and appreciate its warmth and beauty.

We are very excited to have Landauer Publishing join our family here at Fox Chapel Publishing. Their hundreds of quilting titles fit right in with our creative philosophy, and we look forward to publishing more new titles with their roster of well-known quilting experts.

This special issue of *DO Magazine* features an array of quilting projects to use as bedcovers, throws, or wall hangings. Compiled from the works of some of our favorite Landauer authors, you will find unique designs inspired by the mosaic tile floors of Costa Rica (page 3), fun and festive projects to make with your precuts or stash (page 37), a holiday wall hanging using the fast-fold hexie technique (page 92), and how to use the Circle of Nine grid for endless design possibilities (page 17).

Enjoy creating your own quilting story using the projects in this issue. We would love to see what you make, so feel free to send us a photo at editors@domagazines.com.

Melissa

COMMON METRIC CONVERSIONS

(Note: The measurements in this issue do not include the metric equivalents. Refer to this chart to convert the most common measurements to metric.)

¼" = 0.6cm	5" = 12.7cm	⅝ yard = 0.6m
½" = 1.3cm	5½" = 14cm	¾ yard = 0.7m
¾" = 2cm	6" = 15.2cm	1 yard = 0.9m
1" = 2.5cm	6½" = 16.5cm	1½ yards = 1.37m
1¼" = 3.3cm	40" = 1.02m	2 yards = 1.8m
1½" = 3.8cm	41" = 1.04m	2½ yards = 2.3m
1¾" = 4.4cm	42" = 1.07m	3 yard = 2.7m
2" = 5cm	43" = 1.09m	3½ yards = 3.2m
2½" = 6.4cm	44" = 1.12m	4 yards = 3.7m
3" = 7.6cm	⅛ yard = 0.1m	4½ yards = 4.1m
3½" = 8.8cm	¼ yard = 0.2m	5 yards = 4.6m
4" = 10.2cm	½ yard = 0.5m	5½ yards = 5m
4½" = 11.4cm		

DO magazine PRESENTS Quilting TECHNIQUES & PROJECTS

Design Originals Presents Quilting Techniques & Projects
Winter 2018, Volume 4, number 4, issue 14
ISSN 2572-0848

Design Originals: DO Magazine
903 Square Street, Mount Joy, PA 17552
Phone: 717-560-4703 | Fax: 717-560-4702

PUBLISHER	Alan Giagnocavo
VICE PRESIDENT–CONTENT	Christopher Reggio
MANAGING EDITOR	Melissa Younger
CONTRIBUTORS	Patricia Sanabria-Friederich
	Wendy Sheppard
	Janet Houts
	Jean Ann Wright
	McB McManus
	E.B. Updegraff
	Mary M. Hogan
EDITORIAL STAFF	Sue Voegtlin
	Laurel Albright
	Kaitlyn Ocasio
	Llara Pazdan
	Laura Taylor
LAYOUT AND DESIGN STAFF	Wendy Reynolds

ARCHIVAL QUALITY · ACID FREE
200 YEAR PAPER ACID FREE

Newsstand Distribution: Curtis Circulation Company
Circulation Consultant: National Publisher Services
Printed in USA.
©2018 by New Design Originals, Inc. All Rights Reserved.

Images from *Shutterstock.com*: Smaliar Iryna (wood background cover); Nadzin (sewing notion illustrated clipart throughout); Ann.and.Pen (top flower borders project borders throughout); Coprid (2); melnikof (3, 17, 37); elenabsl (34–35 border); Taxiro (34 stitched heart clipart); Seregam (46 bottom); and MaxCab (63 background image; 83).

Mosaic Tile
QUILTING PROJECTS

Patricia Sanabria-Friederich was sitting in church with her mother in her hometown of San Joaquin de Flores, Costa Rica, when she looked down and realized the mosaic tile floor pattern would be ideal for a quilt. She took some photos for reference and began adapting the pattern into a quilt. Soon, she began creating quilts from the mosaics in different churches, schools, and homes throughout Costa Rica.

The quilts in this article were inspired by mosaic tile floors found in Costa Rican churches, schools, and homes. The floors follow the mosaic tile tradition used in Europe. Up until the mid-to-late 1800s, tiles were imported from Europe, but by the early 1900s, Costa Rican craftsmen began creating and designing their own tiles. As tile factories began to open in Costa Rica, more people were able to afford to have these beautiful mosaics in their homes. However, the pigments and molds still came from Europe and the more colorful or complex the design, the more expensive the tile. Thus, there was a correlation between the tile design and the social status of the owner. The building's floor patterns reflect what was in fashion at the time of construction. By the 1940s, mosaic tile floors began to fall out of fashion and were used less and less in newer construction. Some of the tile floor colors have faded over time, especially in buildings more than 70 to 80 years old. To this day, Costa Rica's handmade mosaic tiles are still produced for people who want to keep the traditional-style floors.

Church of El Rosario

I believe there are many similarities between traditional mosaic tile floors and quilts. The tile artist and the quilter both create using molds or patterns, while paying special attention to color combinations and lines. Tile floors and quilts are often put together using a four-block design.

The tradition of mosaic tile design is to create floor patterns when tiles are laid side by side. Coordinating border tiles, which create a rug-like design, often surround the floor pattern. However, a solid color tile may be used to create the floor's border, similar to how we border our quilts.

Tile and quilt makers construct their masterpieces in three layers. Adding colors to a sectioned dye mold creates the mosaic tile. This step relates to a quilter's first layer of piecing. The tile maker then adds the second and third layers of cement prior to the tile being pressed. A quilter uses batting and backing as the second and third layers of her quilt. These three pieces are then quilted.

—Patricia Sanabria-Friederich

Cartago House

Virgen del Carmen Church

Basilica of Santo Domingo Heredia Quilt

BY PATRICIA SANABRIA-FRIEDERICH, FROM HER BOOK *MOSAIC TILE QUILTS*

Santo Domingo is located approximately 4.35 miles (7 km) from Costa Rica's capital city of San Jose. It is a primarily Catholic town influenced by the nineteenth-century economics and architecture of San Jose.

Finished quilt size: 52" x 60¾"
Finished block sizes: 7" x 7" and 1¾" x 1¾"

Materials

+ 1½ yards dark beige fabric
+ ¾ yard gold fabric
+ 1 yard black fabric
+ ¼ yard light beige fabric
+ 1½ yards blue fabric
+ ⅓ yard brown fabric
+ 3¼ yards backing fabric
+ 58" x 67" batting

Note: Quantities are for 40"- to 44"-wide, 100% cotton fabrics. Measurements include ¼" seam allowances. Sew with right sides together unless otherwise stated.

Cut the Fabrics

From dark beige fabric, cut:
+ (12) 4" x 42" strips. From the strips, cut:
  (120) 4" squares for Block 1.

From gold fabric, cut:
+ (13) 1½" x 42" strips. From the strips, cut:
  (360) 1½" squares for Block 1.

From black fabric, cut:
+ (5) 1½" x 42" strips. From the strips, cut:
  (120) 1½" squares for Block 1.
+ (2) 1¾" x 42" strips. From the strips, cut:
  (42) 1¾" center squares for Block 2.
+ (6) 2½" x 42" binding strips. Sew the strips together to make one long strip.

From light beige fabric, cut:
+ (4) 1¾" x 42" strips. From the strips, cut:
  (84) 1¾" squares. Cut each square in half diagonally for a total of 168 triangles for Block 2.

From blue fabric, cut:
+ (15) 2¼" x 42" strips. From the strips, cut:
  (71) 2¼" x 7½" sashing rectangles.
+ (6) 2½" x 42" strips for outer border.

From brown fabric, cut:
+ (6) 1½" x 42" strips for inner border.

From backing fabric, cut:
+ (2) 34" x 58" rectangles.

Block 1 Assembly

1 Draw a diagonal line on the wrong side of the (360) 1½" gold squares and the (120) 1½" black squares.

2 Referring to the diagram, place a 1½" gold square on a corner of a 4" dark beige square, right sides together. Sew on the drawn line. Trim ¼" beyond the stitching line. Press open to reveal a triangle.

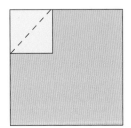 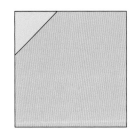

3 Refer to step 2 to add (1) 1½" black square and (2) 1½" gold squares to the remaining corners to complete a snowball unit. Make 120 snowball units.

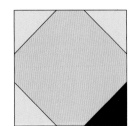

Make 120

4 Lay out 4 snowball units as shown. Join into rows; join rows to complete the block. The block should measure 7½" square. Make 30 Block 1.

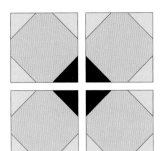 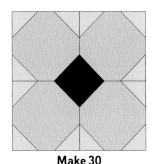

Make 30

Block 2 Assembly

1 Sew (2) 1¾" light beige triangles to opposite sides of a 1¾" black center square. Press seams toward triangles.

2 Sew (2) 1¾" light beige triangles to the remaining sides of the black center square. Press seams toward triangles. If necessary, trim the block to 2¼" square. Make 42 Block 2.

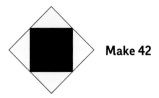

Make 42

Quilt Center Assembly

1 Referring to the Quilt Center Assembly Diagram, lay out 30 Block 1, 42 Block 2, and (71) 2¼" x 7½" blue sashing rectangles in rows as shown.

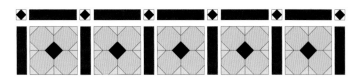

2 Sew the pieces together in rows. You will have (7) Block 2/sashing rectangle rows and (6) Block 1/sashing rectangle rows. Press the seams in each row toward the sashing strips.

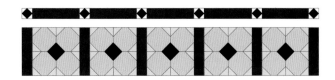

3 Join the rows to make the quilt center. Press seams in one direction.

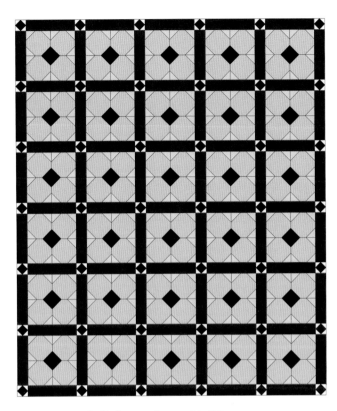

Quilt Center Assembly Diagram

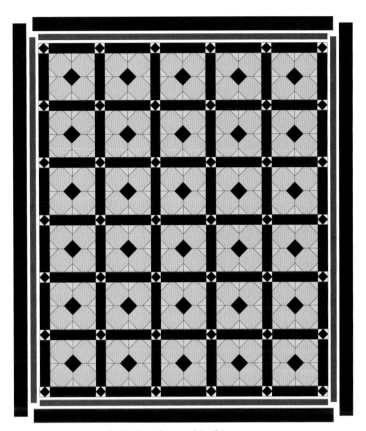

Quilt Top Assembly Diagram

Adding the Inner Border

1. Piece the 1½" x 42" brown inner border strips together into one long strip. From the strip, cut (2) 1½" x 46" top/bottom inner border strips and (2) 1½" x 54¾" side inner border strips.

2. Sew the top/bottom inner border strips to the top and bottom edges of the quilt center. Press seams toward inner border.

3. Sew the side inner border strips to the sides of the quilt center. Press seams toward inner border.

Adding the Outer Border

1. Piece the 2½" x 42" blue outer border strips together into one long strip. From the strip, cut (2) 2½" x 48½" top/bottom outer border strips and (2) 2½" x 60½" side outer border strips.

2. Sew the top/bottom outer border strips to the top and bottom edges of the quilt top. Press seams toward outer border.

3. Sew the side outer border strips to the sides of the quilt top. Press seams toward outer border.

Complete the Quilt

1. Sew the 34" x 58" backing rectangles together along one long edge, using a ½" seam allowance. Press the seam allowance open. Seam will run horizontally across quilt.

2. Layer the quilt top, batting, and pieced backing together.

3. Quilt the layers together.

4. Attach the binding to the outside edges to finish the quilt.

Cartago House Wallhanging

BY PATRICIA SANABRIA-FRIEDERICH, FROM HER BOOK *MOSAIC TILE QUILTS*

This unassuming house, located in the city of Cartago approximately 15 miles (24 km) from San Jose and in the slopes of Irazu volcano, was built around 1910 out of wood. It is believed the home's tile floors were handcrafted locally.

Finished wallhanging size:
34¼" x 43½"

Materials

✢ ¾ yard red fabric
✢ 1 yard blue fabric
✢ 1¼ yards light beige fabric
✢ 1⅜ yards backing fabric
✢ Template plastic
✢ 41" x 50" batting

Quantities are for 40"- to 44"-wide, 100% cotton fabrics. Measurements include ¼" seam allowances. Sew with right sides together unless otherwise stated.

Note: Patterns for Templates A, B, and C are on page 12.

Cut the Fabrics

From red fabric, cut:
✢ (9) Template A.
✢ (6) Template B reversed.

From blue fabric, cut:
✢ (8) Template A reversed.
✢ (8) Template B.
✢ (5) 2½" x 42" binding strips.

From light beige fabric, cut:
✢ (24) Template C.
✢ (4) 3½" x 42" strips. From the strips, cut: (2) 3½" x 37½" and (2) 3½" x 34¼" border strips.

Note: Borders are exact length needed. You may want to cut them longer to allow for differences in piecing.

Wallhanging Center Assembly

1 Referring to Wallhanging Center Assembly Diagram, lay out 9 red A pieces, 6 red B reversed pieces, 8 blue A reversed pieces, 8 blue B pieces, and 24 light beige C pieces in diagonal rows as shown.

2 Sew the pieces together in diagonal rows. Press seams away from the light beige C pieces.

3 Join the diagonal rows to make the wallhanging center. Press seams in one direction.

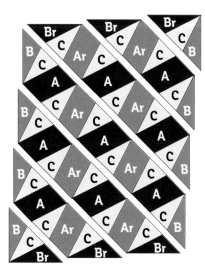

Wallhanging Center Assembly Diagram

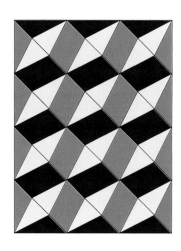

Adding the Border

1 Referring to the Wallhanging Top Assembly
Diagram, sew the light beige 3½" x 37½" border
strips to opposite sides of the wallhanging center.
Press seams toward the border.

2 Sew the light beige print 3½" x 34¼" border strips
to the remaining edges of the wallhanging center.
Press seams toward the border.

Complete the Wallhanging

1 Layer wallhanging top, batting and backing.

2 Quilt as desired.

3 Bind with blue binding strips.

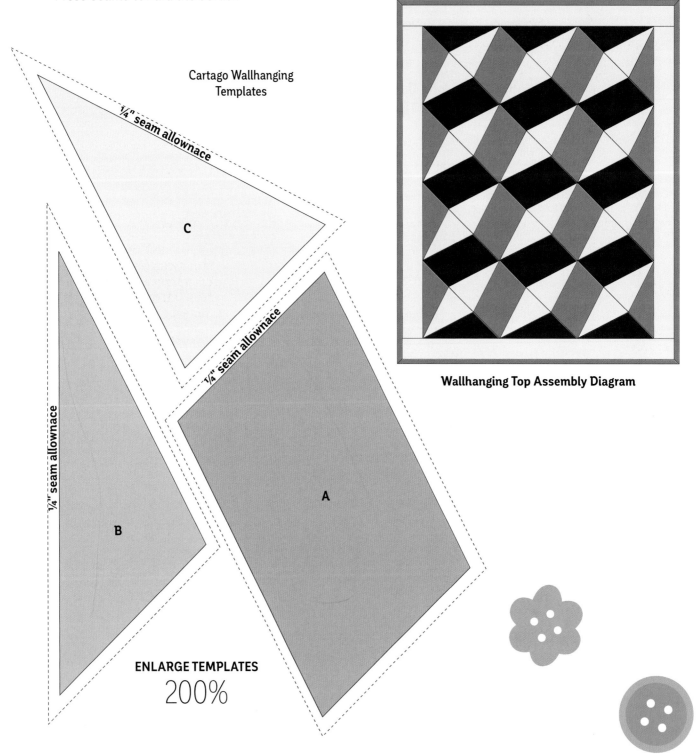

**Cartago Wallhanging
Templates**

¼" seam allownace

C

¼" seam allownace

¼" seam allownace

B

A

ENLARGE TEMPLATES
200%

Wallhanging Top Assembly Diagram

Virgen del Carmen Church Quilt

BY PATRICIA SANABRIA-FRIEDERICH, FROM HER BOOK *MOSAIC TILE QUILTS*

The Virgen del Carmen Church is located in the city of Heredia, Costa Rica, approximately 7.5 miles (12 km) from San Jose. Around 1823 the neighborhood community decided to construct the church to accommodate the growing number of parishioners attending La Inmaculada Concepcion de Maria Church, also located in Heredia, Costa Rica.

Finished size: 57⅜" x 85⅝"
Block sizes: 8½" x 8½" and 5⅝" x 5⅝"

Materials

- ✛ 2½ yards beige fabric
- ✛ 1¼ yards light brown fabric
- ✛ 1 yard off-white fabric
- ✛ 1 yard rust fabric
- ✛ 1 yard black fabric
- ✛ ¾ yard burgundy fabric
- ✛ 5⅛ yards backing fabric
- ✛ 64" x 92" batting

Quantities are for 40"- to 44"-wide, 100% cotton fabrics. Measurements include ¼" seam allowances. Sew with right sides together unless otherwise stated.

Cut the Fabrics

Note: Label the fabric pieces and place in stacks as you are cutting.

From beige fabric, cut:

- ✛ (2) 6⅞" x 42" strips. From the strips, cut: (10) 6⅞" squares. Cut each square diagonally in an X for a total of 40 I triangles for Sashing Units.

Note: There will be 2 extra I triangles.

- ✛ (7) 4½" x 42" strips. From the strips, cut: (24) 4½" x 8½" A rectangles for Block 1 and (7) 4½" D squares for Block 2.
- ✛ (4) 3¾" x 42" strips. From the strips, cut: (38) 3¾" squares. Cut each square in half diagonally for a total of 76 G triangles for Sashing Units.
- ✛ (8) 2½" x 42" strips for border.

From light brown fabric, cut:

- ✛ (4) 6⅞" x 42" strips. From the strips, cut: (19) 6⅞" squares. Cut each square diagonally in an X for a total of 76 H triangles for Sashing Units.
- ✛ (2) 6⅛" x 42" strips. From the strips, cut: (8) 6⅛" J squares for sashing.

From off-white fabric, cut:

- ✛ (4) 6½" x 42" strips. From the strips, cut: (24) 6½" squares. Cut each square in half diagonally for a total of 48 B triangles for Block 1.

From rust fabric, cut:

- ✛ (3) 3¾" x 42" strips. From the strips, cut: (24) 3¾" squares. Cut each square in half diagonally for a total of 48 C triangles for Block 1.
- ✛ (8) 2½" x 42" strips for border.

From black fabric, cut:

- ✛ (2) 3¾" x 42" strips. From the strips, cut: (14) 3¾" squares. Cut each square in half diagonally for a total of 28 E triangles for Block 2.
- ✛ (8) 2½" x 42" binding strips.

From burgundy fabric, cut:

- ✛ (5) 4½" x 42" strips. From the strips, cut: (38) 4½" F squares for sashing.

From backing fabric, cut:

- ✛ (2) 32½" x 92" rectangles.

Block 1 Assembly

1   Sew 2 off-white B triangles to opposite edges of 1 beige A rectangle. Press seams toward triangles.

2   Sew 2 rust C triangles to remaining edges of the rectangle to complete Block 1. Press seams toward triangles. Make 24 Block 1.

Make 24

Block 2 Assembly

1   Sew 2 black E triangles to opposite edges of 1 beige D square. Press seams toward triangles.

2   Sew 2 black E triangles to the remaining edges of the square to complete Block 2. Press seams toward triangles. Make 7 Block 2.

Make 7

Sashing Unit Assembly

1   Lay out 1 burgundy F square, 2 beige G triangles, 2 light brown H triangles, and 1 beige I triangle as shown.

2   Sew the burgundy F square, beige G triangles, and 1 light brown H triangle together. Press seams toward triangles. Sew the remaining light brown H triangle and beige I triangle together. Press seam toward H triangle. Sew the sections together to complete a Sashing Unit. Make 38 Sashing Units.

Make 38

Quilt Center Assembly

1   Referring to the Quilt Center Assembly Diagram, lay out 24 Block 1, 7 Block 2, 38 Sashing Units, and 8 light brown J squares as shown.

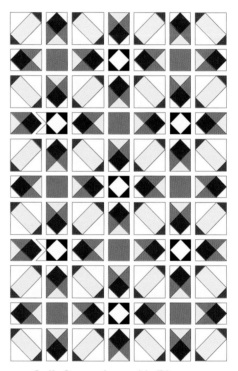

Quilt Center Assembly Diagram

2   Sew the pieces together in each Block 1/sashing row and each sashing/J square/Block 2 row. Press the seams toward the sashing units.

3   Sew the rows together to make the quilt center. Press seams in one direction.

Adding the Border

1 Sew 3 beige 2½" x 42" strips together, end-to-end, to make 1 long strip. Repeat with 3 rust 2½" x 42" strips. Sew the beige and rust strips together along one long edge to make Strip Set 1. Press seam open.

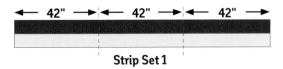

Strip Set 1

2 Square up one end of Strip Set 1. Align the 45-degree line of the ruler with the trimmed end of the strip set. Cut along the ruler's edge, creating a 45-degree angle. Place ruler on strip set, aligning the 3½" line with angled edge of strip. Cut along edge of ruler for Segment 1. Cut 20 Segment 1.

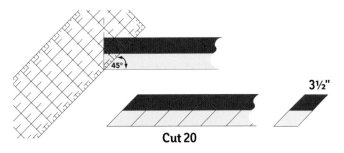

Cut 20

3 Sew together 10 Segment 1 for top border and 10 Segment 1 for bottom border. Sew the pieced borders to top and bottom edges of the quilt center. Press seams toward border. Trim border ends even with side edges of quilt center.

4 Referring to steps 1 and 2, sew (5) 2½" x 42" beige strips and (5) 2½" x 42" rust strips together for Strip Set 2. Cut (32) 3½"-wide Segment 2 as shown.

Cut 20

5 Sew 16 Segment 2 together for 1 side border. Repeat to make 2 side borders. Sew the pieced borders to the side edges of the quilt center. Press seams toward border. Trim side border ends even with the top and bottom edges of the quilt top.

Complete the Quilt

1 Sew the 32½" x 92" backing rectangles together along one long edge, using a ½" seam allowance. Press the seam allowance open.

2 Layer quilt top, batting and pieced backing.

3 Quilt as desired.

4 Bind with black binding strips.

Quilt Top Assembly Diagram

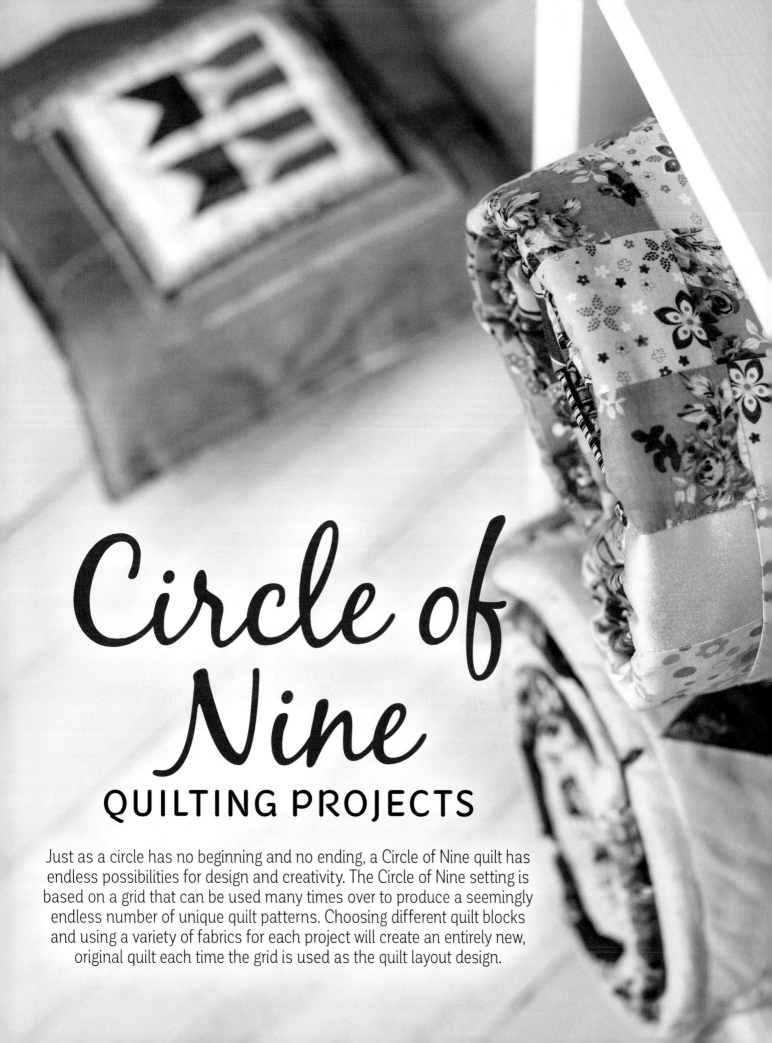

Circle of Nine

QUILTING PROJECTS

Just as a circle has no beginning and no ending, a Circle of Nine quilt has endless possibilities for design and creativity. The Circle of Nine setting is based on a grid that can be used many times over to produce a seemingly endless number of unique quilt patterns. Choosing different quilt blocks and using a variety of fabrics for each project will create an entirely new, original quilt each time the grid is used as the quilt layout design.

Circle of Nine Tools & Techniques

BY JANET HOUTS AND JEAN ANNE WRIGHT, FROM THEIR BOOK *BEST OF CIRCLE OF NINE*

Construction

Designing your own quilts with the Circle of Nine grid is easy! Choose a familiar quilt block and either photocopy it several times or use graph paper to sketch the block. There are endless combinations to put together with blocks and spacers. Just watch the quilt designs multiply with each new choice.

We both carry a pad of graph paper and container of sketching materials with us on vacations, trips to the doctor, etc. We are always ready to create a new quilt when a spare moment presents itself.

Designing quilts on the computer requires either quilt design software or a drawing program. We use both the computer and graph paper sketches, as each method lends a different quality of creativity to the design process. The speed of computer design is very much appreciated, and the relaxing time spent doodling with graph paper can inspire new designs with ease, using the materials at hand.

Draw the blocks using light and dark shading, small dots, stripes, or scribbles to distinguish between different fabric choices. You may also use colored pencils or felt-tip markers.

Sketching Materials

+ Number 2 pencil — This pencil is good for shading, varying from very light to very dark. Inexpensive pencils with an eraser and "push down" lead work very well.

+ Colored pencils or felt-tip markers.

+ Pencil sharpener (I prefer the small, hand-held type).

+ Hand-held eraser — For erasing larger areas easily.

+ Graph paper — 4 or 8 squares to the inch. Each square will represent 1" of fabric. If needed, pages can be taped together to make a larger drawing surface.

+ Quilt block reference books — for choosing blocks to place on the grid. Some good choices are Judy Hopkins's *501 Rotary-Cut Quilt Blocks* and Marsha McClosky's *Block Party* and *Quick & Easy Block Tool*. These books show how to construct the featured blocks.

+ Quilt design computer software can also be used.

Simple Setting

This simple setting produces quilts with unique and creative designs—no two looking alike. The large green squares can be filled with any quilt block. The pink spacers around the center blocks and corner blocks can be a focus fabric or pieced together using traditional block elements.

As we used the Circle of Nine grid more and more as the background for quilt designs, we began to call the areas between the nine arranged blocks "spacers" since these shapes did not behave like quilt blocks or traditional sashings. The word "spacers" soon became a defining term for the Circle of Nine setting.

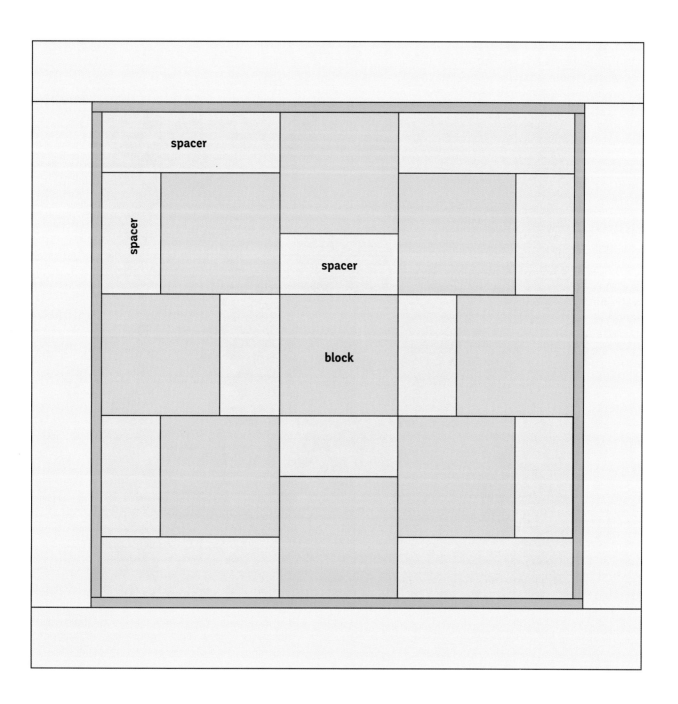

Drafting the Design

Begin by drawing your first quilt block (block 1) at the center of the graph paper. Place block 2 up and to the right of block 1, corner to corner. Place blocks 3, 4, and 5 in the same manner, moving in a clockwise direction. Block 6 will be placed above block 1, halfway between blocks 2 and 5. Blocks 7, 8, and 9 will be placed in the same manner as block 6, rotating clockwise around block 1.

Place spacers around block 1 and in the four corners of the quilt top. These can be made up of strips of fabric (with the top and bottom spacers longer), or smaller quilt block designs. Smaller blocks can also be used in the corners to make all spacers the same size.

TIP:
Use fabric scrap to create your spacers.

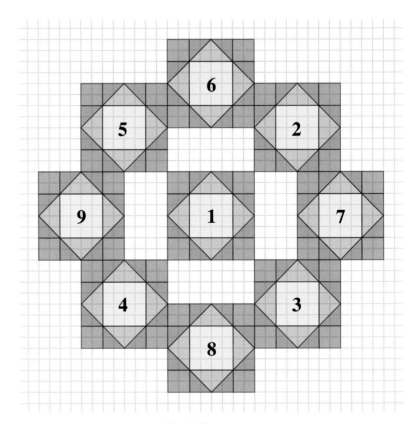

Block Placement

**Alternate Spacer/
Corner Block**

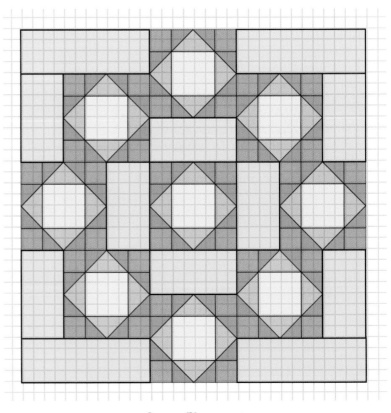

Spacer Placement

Getting Started

A design board of white flannel, quilt batting, or white fleece tacked to a wall is the best way to work with your blocks when creating a Circle of Nine setting. You can position the blocks on the design wall and then step back to view your arrangement before making your spacers and sewing your quilt top together. If space restrictions prohibit the use of a design wall, a good size table or a bed can be used to arrange your blocks.

You need nine finished quilt blocks to make a Circle of Nine setting. You can use nine identical blocks or a combination of two, three, or nine different blocks. Many beautiful Circle of Nine quilts have been made using a collection of nine sampler blocks.

Understanding the Blocks

Most quilt blocks are based on a geometric grid made up of identical size squares. There are some popular exceptions, notably the versatile Square-in-a-Square block.

The most common grids are Square-in-a-Square, One-Patch, Four-Patch, Nine-Patch, and Sixteen-Patch. You can easily count the grid units to see how the blocks get their names.

Square-In-A-Square – used as is, for appliqué, or to put almost any pieced block "on point"

One-Patch – most often used for appliqué or complex blocks like the Mariner's Compass

Four-Patch – used for simple pieced blocks such as Old Maid's Puzzle or Broken Dishes

Nine-Patch – used for star blocks and other more complex designs

Sixteen-Patch – used for many pieced star blocks and blocks using triangles as a design element

Blocks with a square-in-a-square grid have something in common with one-patch, four-patch, and sixteen-patch grids. Each of these blocks fit best in a Circle of Nine setting when they are offset by a half block. The nine-patch grid fits best when offset by one-third or two-thirds so the seams will meet when the blocks are positioned in the Circle of Nine setting.

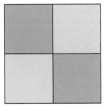

Square-In-A-Square	One-Patch	Four-Patch	Nine-Patch	Sixteen-Patch
6" Blocks	6" Blocks	6" Blocks	6" Blocks	8" Blocks
8" Blocks	8" Blocks	8" Blocks	9" Blocks	10" Blocks
10" Blocks	10" Blocks	10" Blocks	12" Blocks	12" Blocks
12" Blocks	12" Blocks	12" Blocks		

Sample Blocks

Four-Patch Blocks

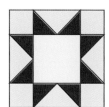

Sawtooth Star

Jack in the Pulpit

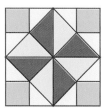

Windmill

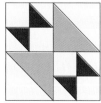

Old Maid's Puzzle

Wedding Ring

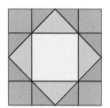

King's Crown

Nine-Patch Blocks

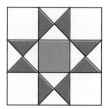

Ohio Star

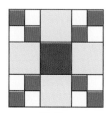

Thrifty

Sailboats

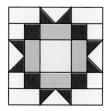

Maple Star

Indiana Puzzle

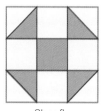

Shoofly

Five-Patch Blocks

Bear Paw

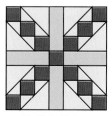

Buffalo Ridge

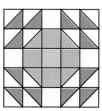

Crown of Thorns

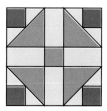

Grandmother's Choice

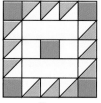

Zigzag

Using Spacers

Spacers are the units that pull the nine blocks in a Circle of Nine quilt setting together. The grid division of the nine quilt blocks will determine the size of the spacers. Seamlines can be aligned and the height of a spacer rectangle can be one-half, one-third, or one-fourth the size of the quilt block.

You might wish to cut some fabric scraps into squares, triangles, or strips to audition how they look with your nine blocks. If you use pieced spacers, you can turn them in the opposite direction, which often creates an entirely different quilt design. Some examples of spacer choices are shown. The below images have spacer diagrams to illustrate some suggested designs for various sized quilt blocks.

**The same quilt block setting with spacers
turned in the opposite direction.**

**The same quilt block setting with spacers
of different pieced designs.**

Sewing the Spacer Units

There are four basic units that are used over and over again in the various spacers. Learning how to make these units in various sizes will prove useful as you design your own Circle of Nine quilts. Variations may also be used from time to time, so learning the basics is important.

Half-Square Triangles

1 Cut 1 light-color square and 1 dark-color square.

2 Place the light-color square on the dark-color square, right sides together. Draw a diagonal line from corner to corner on the wrong side of the light-color square.

3 Stitch ¼" on either side of the drawn line.

4 Cut the square apart on the marked line to make two half-square triangles.

5 Fold the cut units open and press the seam line to complete a half-square triangle unit.

6 Press both seams toward the darker fabric. Trim away any seam allowance "tails" to square up the units.

Quarter-Square Triangles

1 Cut 1 light-color square and 1 dark-color square.

2 Place the light-color square on the dark-color square, right sides together. Draw a diagonal line from corner to corner in both directions to make an "X" on the wrong side of the light-color square.

3 Stitch a scant ¼" on either side of one of the marked lines. Cut apart on the drawn line between the stitched lines. Cut apart on the other marked line without stitching.

4 Press seams toward the dark triangle on the resulting four double-triangle units.

5 Position the triangles, right sides together, with light triangle on dark triangle. Stitch together along the long edge using a scant ¼" seam allowance.

6 Fold the quarter-square triangle units open and press the seam line to complete two quarter-square triangle units.

Flying Geese

1 Cut 1 dark rectangle and 2 light-color squares.

2 Draw a diagonal line from corner to corner on the wrong side of the light-color squares.

3 Place a marked light-color square even with one end of the dark rectangle, right sides together. Sew on the diagonal line.

4 Cut away the excess fabric ¼" from the stitching line.

5 Fold out the resulting triangle and press the seam line.

6 Repeat with the remaining light-color square on the opposite side of the dark rectangle.

7 Cut away the excess fabric ¼" from the stitching line.

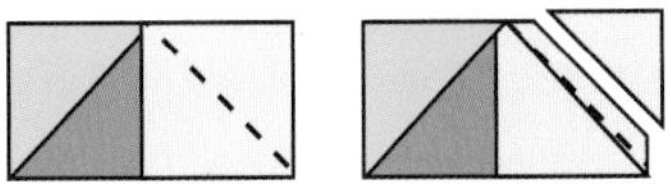

8 Fold out the resulting triangle and press the seam line to complete the flying geese unit.

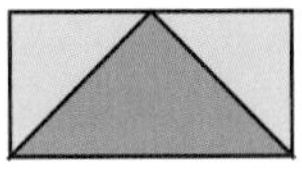

Square-in-a-Square

1 Cut 1 dark fabric square and 4 small light-color squares.

2 Draw a diagonal line from corner to corner on the wrong side of the light-color squares.

3 Place a marked light-color square in opposite corners of the dark-color square, right sides together. Stitch on the drawn lines.

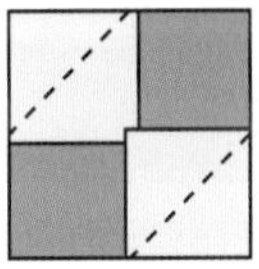

4 Cut away the excess fabric ¼" from the stitching line on each of the (2) small squares. Fold out the resulting triangles and press the seam lines.

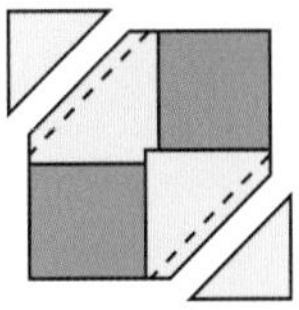

5 Repeat with the remaining light-color squares on the remaining corners of the dark square.

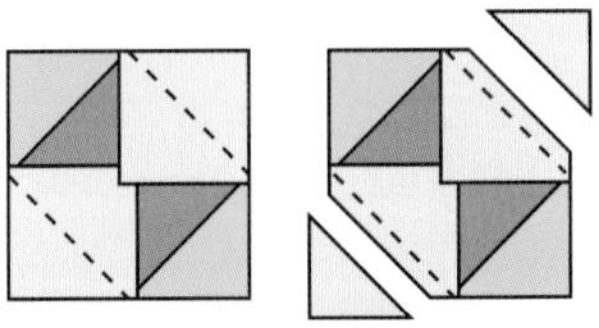

6 Cut away the excess fabric ¼" from the stitched lines. Fold out the resulting triangles and press the seam line to complete the square-in-a-square unit.

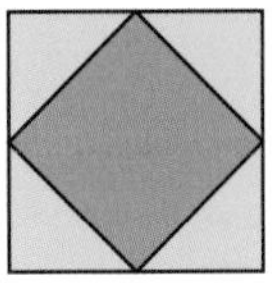

HALF-SQUARE TRIANGLES

Add ⅞" to finished size of half-square triangle units

Unit size	Cut size	From 1 WOF strip
2"	2⅞" squares	cut 14
3"	3⅞" squares	cut 10
4"	4⅞" squares	cut 8
5"	5⅞" squares	cut 7
6"	6⅞" squares	cut 6

QUARTER-SQUARE TRIANGLES

Add 1¼" to finished size of quarter-square triangle units

Unit size	Cut size	From 1 WOF strip
3"	4¼" squares	cut 9
4"	5¼" squares	cut 8
5"	6¼" squares	cut 6
6"	7¼" squares	cut 6

FLYING GEESE

Unit size	Cut size	From 1 WOF strip
2" x 4"	2½" x 4½" rectangles	cut 9
	2½" squares	cut 16
2½" x 5"	3" x 5½" rectangles	cut 7
	3" squares	cut 14
3" x 6"	3½" x 6½" rectangles	cut 6
	3½" squares	cut 12

SQUARE-IN-A-SQUARE

Unit size	Cut size	From 1 WOF strip
3"	3½" squares	cut 12
	2" squares	cut 20
4"	4½" squares	cut 9
	2½" squares	cut 16
5"	5½" squares	cut 7
	3" squares	cut 14
6"	6½" squares	cut 6
	3½" squares	cut 12

Garden Pinwheels Quilt

BY JANET HOUTS & JEAN ANN WRIGHT, FROM THEIR BOOK *BEST OF CIRCLE OF NINE*

Finished size: 63" x 63"
Block size: 12"

Fabric collection: Flower Doodle by Kim Schaefer for Andover Fabrics
WOF = Width of fabric
LOF = Length of fabric

NOTE: Sew all blocks with a scant ¼" seam.

Materials

- ✦ Fabric A—2 yards large-scale allover floral print (borders, spacer corners)
- ✦ Fabric B—¾ yard red texture print (borders, binding)
- ✦ Fabric C—1 yard white with black figures print (spacers, borders)
- ✦ Fabric D—¾ yard black geometric print (spacers)
- ✦ Fabric E—½ yard teal blue print (blocks)
- ✦ Fabric F—½ yard lavender print (blocks)
- ✦ Fabric G—½ yard yellow texture print (blocks)
- ✦ Fabric H—½ yard red geometric print (blocks)
- ✦ Backing—4 yards

Cut the Fabrics

From Fabric A, cut:

- ✦ (1) 6½" x WOF strip; from this strip cut:
  (4) 6½" squares for spacer corners
- ✦ (4) 6½" x LOF strips for borders; from these strips cut: (2) 6½" x 51½" side borders and (2) 6½" x 63½" top/bottom borders

From Fabric B, cut:

- ✦ (5) 2" x WOF strips; sew together end-to-end and cut:
  (2) 2" x 48½" side borders and (2) 2" x 51½" top/bottom borders
- ✦ (6) 2¼" x WOF strips; sew together end-to-end to make binding

From Fabric C, cut:

- ✦ (5) 1½" x WOF strips; sew together end-to-end and cut:
  (4) 1½" x 51½" strips for folded flange
- ✦ (4) 6½" x WOF strips; from these strips cut:
  (12) 6½" x 12½" rectangles for spacers

From Fabric D, cut:

- ✦ (4) 6½" x WOF strips; from these strips cut: (24) 6½" squares

From Fabric E, cut:

- ✦ (4) 3½" x WOF strips; from these strips cut: (36) 3½" squares

From Fabric F, cut:

- ✦ (4) 3⅞" x WOF strips; from these strips cut: (36) 3⅞" squares; cut in half once on the diagonal to make (72) half-square triangles

From Fabric G, cut:

- ✦ (2) 7¼" x WOF strips from these strips cut: (9) 7¼" squares; cut in half twice on the diagonal to make (36) quarter-square triangles

From Fabric H, cut:

- ✦ (2) 7¼" x WOF strips from these strips cut: (9) 7¼" squares; cut in half twice on the diagonal to make (36) quarter-square triangles

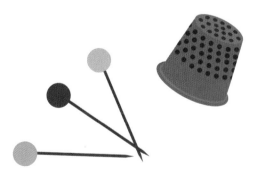

Block Assembly

1   Sew a Fabric G quarter-square triangle and a Fabric H quarter-square triangle together along the long side to make a square unit. Make 36 units.

Make 36

2   Sew four units from step 1 together to make a pinwheel unit. Make 9 units.

Make 9

3   Sew a Fabric F half-square triangle to each side of a Fabric E square to make a triangle unit. Make 36 units.

Make 36

4   Sew four triangle units from step 3 to each side of the pinwheel units made in step 2 to complete a block. Make 9 blocks.

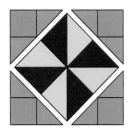
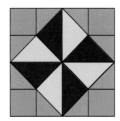

Make 9

Spacer Assembly

Draw a diagonal line on wrong side of all Fabric D 6½" squares. Place a marked square on the left side of a Fabric C 6½" x 12½" rectangle, right sides together. Sew on the diagonal line. Trim ¼" from stitched line and press the corner triangle open. Repeat on the opposite side of the rectangle to make a flying geese spacer unit. Make 12.

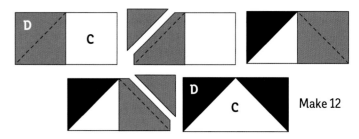

Make 12

Section Assembly

1   Refer to Quilt Assembly Diagram on the following page for block and spacer placement. Pay close attention to the orientation of blocks and spacers as you sew each section.

2   Center section: Sew a flying geese spacer unit to top and bottom of a block. Sew a block to top and bottom of the flying geese spacers to complete the center section.

3   Outside sections: Sew a flying geese spacer to one side of the remaining blocks, referring to the Quilt Assembly Diagram for orientation of the spacers. Sew a Fabric A 6½" square to one end of the remaining four flying geese spacers. Assemble the two outside sections, referring to the Quilt Assembly Diagram.

4   Sew the outside sections to opposite sides of the center section to complete the quilt center.

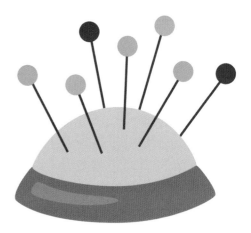

Border Assembly

Refer to Quilt Assembly Diagram below to add borders.

1 Sew the Fabric B 2" x 48½" side borders to opposite sides of the quilt center.

2 Sew the Fabric B 2" x 51½" top/bottom borders to the top and bottom of the quilt center.

3 Fold the Fabric C 1½" x 51½" strips in half lengthwise with wrong sides together. Press fold line. Place the folded flange strip, with raw edges together, to the top Fabric B border strip. Top stitch ⅛" from raw edges to baste the flange in place. Repeat on the opposite border and then the top and bottom borders until all four sides are basted.

4 Sew the Fabric A 6½" x 51½" side borders to opposite sides of the quilt top. Sew the Fabric A 6½" x 63½" top/bottom strips to the top and bottom of the quilt center to complete the quilt top.

Finishing the Quilt

Layer the quilt backing fabric, batting, and quilt top. Baste the layers together. Hand or machine quilt as desired. Bind to finish the quilt.

Quilt Assembly Diagram

Upstairs, Downstairs Quilt

BY JANET HOUTS & JEAN ANN WRIGHT, FROM THEIR BOOK *BEST OF CIRCLE OF NINE*

Finished size: 68" x 68"
Block size: 12"

Fabric collection: Baby Safari by
   Carina Gardner for Benartex
WOF = Width of fabric
LOF = Length of fabric

*NOTE: Sew all blocks with a scant
¼" seam.*

Materials

✦ Fabric A—1½ yards multicolor
   circles print (blocks)
✦ Fabric B—1½ yards green
   swirls print (blocks, corner
   spacers)
✦ Fabric C—⅝ yard cream
   (spacers)
✦ Fabric D—¾ yard orange print
   (spacers, binding)
✦ Fabric E—¼ yard blue dots
   print (spacers)
✦ Fabric F—½ yard small green
   print (inside borders)
✦ Fabric G—2 yards large plaid
   print (outside borders)
✦ Backing—4¼ yards

Cut the Fabrics

From Fabric A, cut:

✦ (3) 12½" x WOF strips; from these strips cut: (9) 12½" squares

From Fabric B, cut:

✦ (7) 6½" x WOF strips; from these strips cut: (40) 6½" squares

From Fabric C, cut:

✦ (2) 6½" x WOF strips; from these strips cut: (12) 6½" squares
✦ (1) 3½" x WOF strip; from this strip cut: (12) 3½" squares

From Fabric D, cut:

✦ (2) 3⅞" x WOF strips; from these strips cut:
   (12) 3⅞" squares, cut in half once on the diagonal to make
   (24) half-square triangles
✦ (7) 2¼" x WOF strips; sew together end-to-end to make binding

From Fabric E, cut:

✦ (1) 6⅞" x WOF strip; from this strip cut:
   (6) 6⅞" squares, cut in half once on the diagonal to make
   (12) half-square triangles

From Fabric F, cut:

✦ (5) 2½" x WOF strips; sew together end-to-end and cut:
   (2) 2½" x 48½" side borders and
   (2) 2½" x 52½" top/bottom borders

From Fabric G, cut:

✦ (4) 8½" x LOF strips; from these strips cut:
   (2) 8½" x 52½" side borders and
   (2) 8½" x 68½" top/bottom borders

Block Assembly

Draw a diagonal line on wrong side of all Fabric B 6½" squares. Place a marked square on the upper left corner of a Fabric A 12½" square, right sides together. Sew on the diagonal line. Trim ¼" from stitched line and press the corner triangle open. Repeat for remaining 3 corners. Make 9.

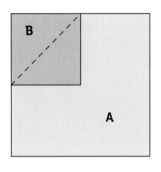

Make 9

Spacer Assembly

Sew a Fabric D half-square triangle to the left and bottom edges of a Fabric C 3½" square to make a D/C unit. Sew a Fabric E 6⅞" half-square triangle to the D/C unit to make a D/C/E unit. Sew the D/C/E unit to a Fabric C 6½" square to make a spacer unit. Make 12.

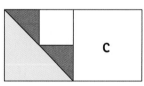

Make 12

Section Assembly

1. Refer to Quilt Assembly Diagram on the next page for block and spacer placement. Pay close attention to the orientation of spacer/block units as you sew each section.

2. Center section: Sew a spacer unit to top and bottom of a block. Sew a block to top and bottom of the spacer units to complete the center section.

3. Outside sections: Sew a spacer unit to one side of each of the remaining blocks. Sew spacer/block units together as shown in the Quilt Assembly Diagram. Pay careful attention to orientation of spacer units to create the correct "stair step" direction.

4. Paying careful attention to direction of triangle units, sew a Fabric B 6½" square to one side of remaining 4 spacer units. Sew to top and bottom of outside sections.

5. Sew the outside sections to opposite sides of the center section to complete the quilt center.

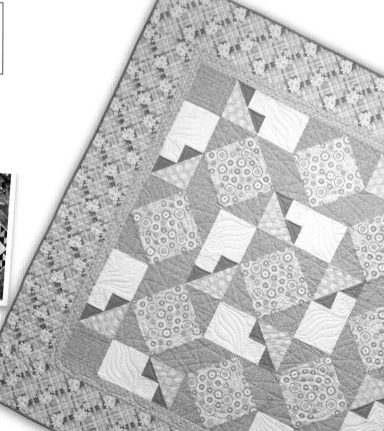

Border Assembly

Refer to Quilt Assembly Diagram below to add borders.

1. Sew the Fabric F 2½" x 48½" side borders to opposite sides of the quilt center. Sew the Fabric F 2½" x 52½" top/bottom borders to the top and bottom of the quilt center.

2. Sew the Fabric G 8½" x 52½" side borders to opposite sides of the quilt top. Sew the Fabric G 8½" x 68½" top/bottom borders to the top and bottom of the quilt center to complete the quilt top.

Finishing the Quilt

Layer the quilt backing fabric, batting, and quilt top. Baste the layers together. Hand or machine quilt as desired. Bind to finish the quilt.

Quilt Assembly Diagram

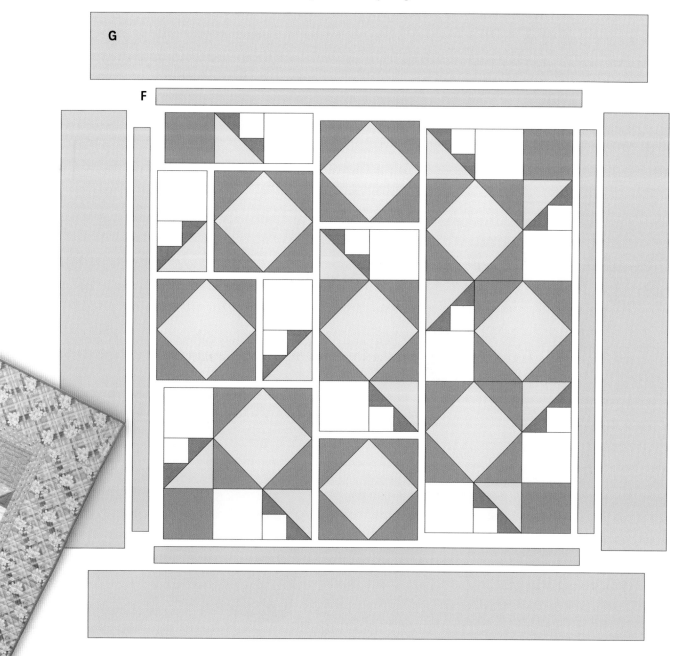

We're LOVING It!

It's time to cozy up by the fire under a cushy new quilt, crafted by you!

With the chill of winter already in the air, what better time to hone your skills and create the ideal quilt? Below are some items we think are pretty *cool*, and perfect for a snowy day project! Get ready to snuggle up with these great ideas.

Traveling at a Good Clip

This snipper cuts thread, yarn, and embroidery floss like butter. It features a retractable cord and clip for tangle-free use and portability. A built-in LED light is handy for hard-to-see angles and low-light conditions. The locking safety feature protects the serrated cutting blades. It's the perfect cutting solution for use on the go!

Thread Cutterz Snipper
$16.99, *www.threadcutterz.com*

CLIP & LED LIGHT!

A Cut above the Rest

This rotary cutter packs a big punch at a small size! At only 1.75" x 2.25", its straight-edge blade can easily cut up to eight layers of quilter's cotton, making it the perfect companion for any busy quilter. It features a safety lock that keeps it closed when you're on the move, and open and in place when you're sewing. The textured grips on the handle and ribbed finger rest help you keep a firm grip as you work. **Crafter's bonus:** it can be used for cutting paper as well!

Dritz® Travel Rotary Cutter
$6.99, *www.fatquartershop.com*

Impressive Results

This flexible mat allows you to press any pieced or embroidered block with ease. The density of this high-quality 100% felted wool mat absorbs seams and stitches, effectively pressing both sides at once. Knitted projects can be blocked by pinning them directly to the mat. The texture of the wool stops fabrics from shifting so there is no distortion when pressing, and it can be used with a dry iron on any surface. Mat sizes range from 4" square up to 17" x 24"—perfect for projects of any size!

Gypsy™ Felted Wool Pressing Mat
$19.99 (8.5" x 8.5" size), *www.gypsyquilter.com*

Guiding the Way

This guide helps you set your sewing machine needle for your desired seam size. The see-through plastic make it easy to position your machine's needle exactly where you need it, as well as to double-check the accuracy of your needle's position. The unique 45-degree mitered end is handy for piecing binding strips together.

CutRite™ Sewing Machine Seam Guide
$1.95, *www.quiltersparadiseesc.com*

EASY & ACCURATE!

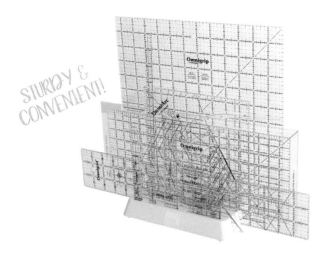

STURDY & CONVENIENT!

Stand and Deliver

No more endlessly searching for where you set down your ruler! This ruler stand is made of sturdy plastic and helps keep rulers and templates organized and in easy reach. The ten slots are wide enough to accommodate ⅛"–thick rulers and templates. This sturdy storage solution features rubber feet for grip to your work surface as well as built-in slots on the back for a flush wall mount.

Dritz® Quilting Ruler Stand
$19.99, *www.joann.com*

New Kid on the Block

Give your calculator a break with this handy tool! You can now create square-on-square blocks with ease—all of the cutting measurements are printed right on the tool! The ruler slides easily over the fabric until pressure is applied, and the exclusive gripper holds the fabric in place while cutting, eliminating slipping and miss-cuts. Trimming each round as triangles are added creates perfectly square, uniform blocks. Plus, it's available in multiple sizes, so the only limitation is your imagination! **Bonus:** The popular "Snail's Trail" block is now easier than ever—simply change the colors of the triangles!

**Creative Grids®
Square-on-Square Trim Tool**
$22.49 (8.5" x 8.5" size),
www.creativegridsusa.com

Quilt Block Pattern Packs *from*  Quilted Fox Designs

Inspirational Block Designs
for Contemporary and Traditional
Quilt Makers

- Simple & Easy Patterns with Step-by-Step Instructions
- Complete Materials List on Back Cover
- Featuring Today's Most Popular Quilt Block Designs

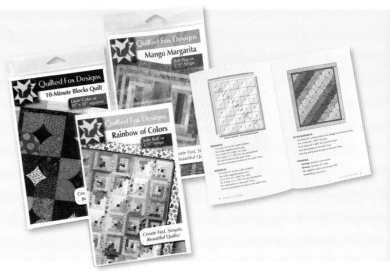

10-Minute Blocks Quilt
$9.00 • #DO8186

Quilt & Learn Table Runner
$9.00 • #DO8188

Motion Commotion
$9.00 • #DO8187

Cotton Candy
$9.00 • #DO8195

Rainbow of Colors
$9.00 • #DO8191

Zen-Sational Butterfly Blocks
$9.00 • #DO8189

Mango Margarita Pattern
$9.00 • #DO8190

Sunrise Batiks Pattern
$9.00 • #DO8193

Tutti Frutti Pattern
$9.00 • #DO8194

Lemongrass Pattern
$9.00 • #DO8192

* FREE SHIPPING with your order!
Regular shipping and handling is FREE for all orders shipped within the USA. **Use coupon code DOQ18 after placing item in cart or when ordering.** Offer expires 01/31/19. For orders shipped outside the USA, you will receive a discount equal to the US shipping cost and we will bill you the difference.

By Phone: 800-457-9112 • Direct: 717-560-4703
Fax: 717-560-4702
Online at: www.FoxChapelPublishing.com
By Mail: Send Check or Money Order to
Fox Chapel Publishing
903 Square St.
Mount Joy, PA 17552

DESIGN ORIGINALS

Precuts & Stash

QUILTING PROJECTS

Precut fabric bundles are one of the biggest buzzes in the quilting world. The major draw to these convenient bundles is they are conducive to fast and easy cutting for the quick completion of quilt projects. In addition to being creatively packaged, they also give quilters a chance to enjoy all the fabrics in one line. More fabrics automatically means scrappier quilts, which most quilters are delightfully obsessed with.

orking with precut fabrics is very convenient for me. I always tend to cut my non-precut fabrics into smaller, more manageable pieces before I start cutting pieces for my quilt projects. Precuts always save me a few extra steps in cutting, especially the 2½" strips which I love to use to make my binding strips.

Precuts from your stash

There is no written rule that says you have to use all the precut fabric pieces within a bundle. In fact, most quilt projects will NOT use every fabric in the bundle. You will end up with precut pieces in your fabric stash, so why not store your leftover precut pieces for future projects? I have heard from many quilters who cut their leftover fabrics into convenient sizes, store and label them to make their own precut fabric stash. What a fantastic idea! Some of the projects in this book were made with precut scraps from my stash.

In *Creative New Quilts & Projects from Precuts or Stash*, I have sought to interject more design elements, as well as possibilities, into precuts projects.

I attempted to keep the projects non-fabric specific, which makes personalizing the quilt projects so much easier and fun. If fabric lines were used, the names are listed in the project instructions, but quilters can easily pull leftovers from previous precut bundles for any of the projects. The fabrics listed in the instructions can easily be changed, based on what you have in your stash. For example, when a fat quarter is listed in the supplies list, substitute with a variety of 5" or 10" squares.

Changing the size of the projects

The projects in this book offer a variety of sizes, from a hanging banner to a bed quilt. However, each project can easily be made larger or smaller by either changing the block size or the number of blocks.

There are a few simple appliqué projects included to illustrate that precuts are versatile for any type of project. While many quilters use scraps to add a multitude of colors to their appliqué projects, I treat the small precut fabrics as "scraps" when I audition fabrics for my appliqué projects.

Precut fabric bundles have brought such fun and excitement to quilters, and I believe they will continue to do so for a long time. With that in mind, it is my hope that you will enjoy using your precut bundles to make the projects in *Creative New Quilts & Projects from Precuts or Stash*.

Quiltingly yours,
Wendy Sheppard

Fat Quarter 18" x 22" piece of fabric	**Fat Eighth** 9" x 22" piece of fabric
2½" x WOF Strips Common names: Jelly Roll, Roll Ups, Pops, Rolie Polies, Pixie Strips, Strips	**5" Fabric Squares** Common names: Charms, Snaps, Minis, 5" Stackers, Chips, Stamps
10" Fabric Squares Common names: Layer Cakes, Crackers, Ten Squares, Patty Cakes, Squares, 10" Stackers, Tiles, Stacks	**Triangles** Common names: Turnovers, HST (half-square triangles)
1½" x WOF Strips Common names: Honey Buns, Skinny Strips, Rolie Polies	**2½" Squares** Common names: Candies, Mini Charms
5" x 44" Strips Common names: Dessert Roll, Twice the Charm, Fat Rolls, Charm Rolls	**6" Hexagons** Common names: Hexies, Honeycombs

Gwendolyn's Dream Garden Quilt

BY WENDY SHEPPARD, FROM HER BOOK *CREATIVE NEW QUILTS & PROJECTS FROM PRECUTS OR STASH*

Finished block size: 12" square
Finished quilt size: 78" x 90"

Materials

Note: I used fabrics from the Hello Darling collection by Moda. The design is perfect for using leftover precuts or an assortment of fabrics from your stash.

- 5 or more assorted fat quarters OR (72) 5" charm squares for Block A
- (33) 2½" x WOF white solid strips for Blocks A and B OR Jelly Roll bundle of white strips
- 40 or more 2½" x WOF assorted print strips for Blocks A and B OR Jelly Roll bundle of assorted prints
- 28 or more assorted print fat quarters OR (62) 10" squares for Block B
- 1⅞ yards white solid fabric for sashing and border strips
- (10) 2½" x WOF print strips for binding
- 84" x 96" backing fabric
- 84" x 96" batting fabric
- WOF = width of fabric Sew with ¼" seam allowance unless otherwise noted. Read through all instructions before beginning this project.

Cut the Fabrics

From 5 or more assorted fat quarters OR (72) 5" charm squares, cut:

- (72) 4½" squares for Block A

Note: 18 sets of matching 4½" squares were used in the featured quilt.

From 12 white solid 2½" x WOF strips, cut:

- (180) 2½" squares for Block A

From 4 white solid 2½" x WOF strips, cut:

- (68) 2" squares for Block B

From 13 white solid 2½" x WOF strips, cut:

- (204) 2½" squares for Block B half-square triangle units

From 12 or more assorted print 2½" x WOF strips, cut:

- (180) 2½" print squares for Block A

From 28 or more assorted print 2½" x WOF strips, cut:

- (221) 2½" squares for Block B
- (34) 2" x 6½" rectangles for Block B
- (34) 2" x 9½" rectangles for Block B

From 28 or more assorted print fat quarters OR (62) 10" squares, cut:

- (17) 1½" x 2½" rectangles for Block B
- (34) 1½" x 3½" rectangles for Block B
- (34) 1½" x 4½" rectangles for Block B
- (34) 1½" x 5½" rectangles for Block B
- (17) 1½" x 6½" rectangles for Block B

From white solid fabric, cut:

- (17) 3½" x WOF strips. Sew the strips together along the short ends to make one continuous strip.
  From the strip, cut:
  (4) 3½" x 84½" sashing strips
  (2) 3½" x 78½" top/bottom border strips
  (2) 3½" x 84½" side border strips

Block Assembly

Block A

1 Lay out (2) 2½" white solid and (2) 2½" assorted print squares as shown. Sew the squares together to make a four-patch unit. Make 5 four-patch units.

Make 5

2 Lay out 5 four-patch units and (4) 4½" squares as shown. Sew the pieces together to complete Block A. Make 18 Block A.

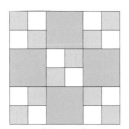

Make 18

Block B

1 Draw a diagonal line on the wrong side of a 2½" assorted print square. With right sides together, place the marked square on a 2½" white solid square. Stitch ¼" on either side of the drawn line.

2 Cut on drawn line. Press open to make 2 half-square triangle units. Make 24 half-square triangle units. Line up the diagonal seam of the half-square triangle units with the 45-degree line on a ruler. Trim the units to 2" square. Make 24 half-square triangle units.

 Make 24

3 Lay out a 1½" x 2½" print rectangle and a 2½" print square as shown. Sew the pieces together.

4 Sew a 1½" x 3½" print rectangle to the top of the unit in step 3. Sew a 1½" x 3½" print rectangle to the left side of the unit.

5 Sew a 1½" x 4½" print rectangle to the bottom of the unit in step 4.

6 Continuing in a counter-clockwise direction, sew a 1½" x 4½" print rectangle, (2) 1½" x 5½" print rectangles, and a 1½" x 6½" print rectangle to the sewn unit.

7 Sew 2" x 6½" print rectangles to opposite sides of the sewn unit. Sew 2" x 9½" print rectangles to the remaining sides of the sewn unit to complete a Block B center.

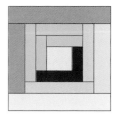

8 Lay out 6 half-square triangle units in a row. Sew the units together to make a column. Make 4 columns.

9 Sew 2 columns to opposite sides of the Block B center.

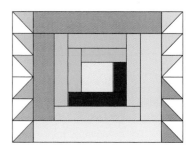

10 Sew a 2" white solid square to the opposite sides of the remaining columns. Sew the columns to the top and bottom of the Block B center to complete Block B. Make a total of 17 Block B.

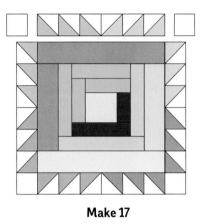

Make 17

Quilt Top Assembly

1 Referring to the Quilt Center Assembly Diagram below, lay out blocks A and B in five columns as shown.

2 Sew the blocks together in columns.

3 Lay out the five columns and (4) 3½" x 84½" sashing strips as shown.

4 Sew the pieces together to complete the quilt top center.

5 Sew 3½" x 84½" side border strips to opposite sides of the quilt center.

6 Sew 3½" x 78½" top/bottom border strips to the top/bottom of the quilt center to complete the quilt top.

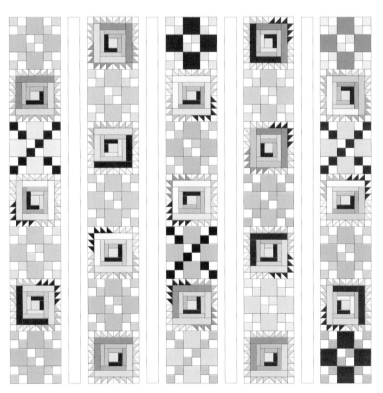

Quilt Center Assembly Diagram

Finishing

1 Lay the backing fabric, wrong side up, on a flat surface. The backing fabric should be taut. Place the batting on the backing and the quilt top on the batting, right side up, to form a quilt sandwich. Baste the quilt sandwich.

2 Quilt as desired.

Quilting notes: Allover swirl/petal motifs were quilted over the entire quilt top.

3 Sew the (10) 2½" x WOF binding strips together along the short ends to make one continuous binding strip. Fold the piece in half lengthwise, wrong sides together, and press. Sew to the raw edge of the quilt top. Fold the binding over the raw edges and hand stitch in place on back of quilt.

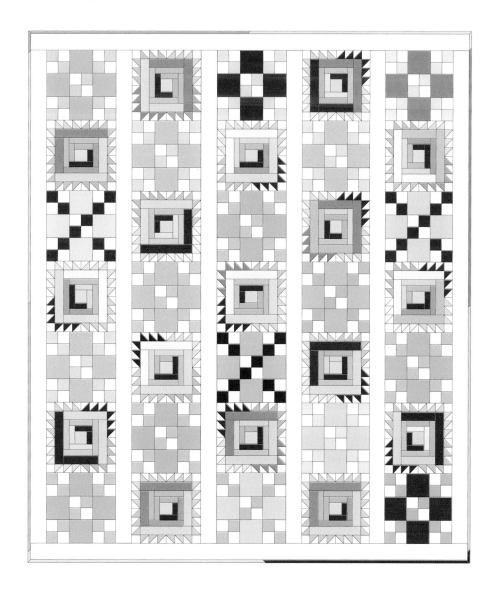

Birds of a Feather Place Mats

BY WENDY SHEPPARD, FROM HER BOOK *CREATIVE NEW QUILTS & PROJECTS FROM PRECUTS OR STASH*

Finished place mat size:
16½" x 12"
Makes 2 place mats

Materials

Note: I used The Sweet Life by Pat Sloan for Moda. If you're using a jelly roll bundle, you will have enough strips left for the appliqués and another set of place mats.

+ 1 fat quarter focal fabric
+ 1 jelly roll bundle OR an assortment of (18) 2½" x WOF strips
+ 2 fat quarters backing fabric
+ (2) 16" x 20" pieces batting
+ Optional appliqué: 3 fat quarters
+ Fat Quarter = 18" x 22"
+ Jelly Roll strip = 2½" x WOF
+ WOF = width of fabric

Sew with ¼" seam allowance unless otherwise noted.

Cut the Fabrics

From focal fabric fat quarter, cut:
+ (2) 10½" x 12½" rectangles

From (2) assorted 2½" WOF strips, cut:
+ (4) 1¼" x 12½" sashing rectangles

From assorted 2½" WOF strips, cut:
+ (12) 2½" x 5½" rectangles

From 3 fat quarters for optional appliqué, cut:
+ Appliqué shapes on page 47

Place Mat Assembly

1 Sew (6) 2½" x 5½" assorted rectangles together along the long edges to make a column.

2 Sew (2) 1¼" x 12½" sashing rectangles together along one long edge.

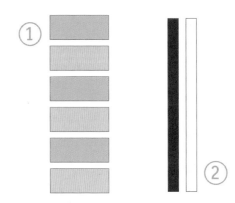

3 Sew the sashing rectangles from step 2 to the right side of the column from step 1.

4 Sew a 10½" x 12½" focal fabric rectangle to the remaining side of the sashing rectangle to complete one place mat top.

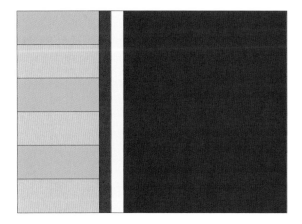

5 Lay the backing fabric, wrong side up, on a flat surface. The backing fabric should be taut. Layer batting and place mat top, right side up, on top of backing to form a sandwich. Baste the sandwich.

6 Quilt as desired.

7 Sew (2) 2½" x WOF strips together along the short ends to make one continuous strip for binding. Fold the piece in half lengthwise, wrong sides together, and press. Sew to the raw edge of the place mat top. Fold the binding over the raw edges and hand stitch in place on back of place mat.

8 Repeat the steps to make another place mat.

Optional Appliqué

Prepare the appliqué shapes using your favorite method. Fusible appliqué was used on the featured place mats. Referring to the diagrams and the photo on the next page, arrange the prepared appliqué pieces on the place mat top. Sew the pieces in place using a favorite appliqué stitch.

Templates

Branch
Template

Bird
Template

Templates have
been reversed for
fusible appliqué

Color Options

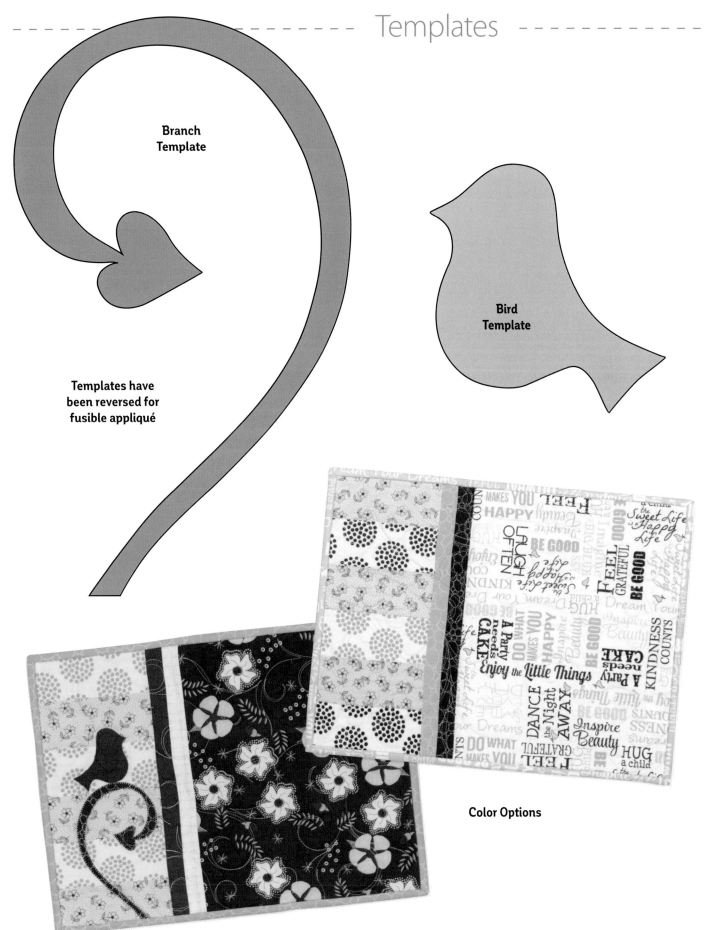

Winter Blues Quilt

BY WENDY SHEPPARD, FROM HER BOOK *CREATIVE NEW QUILTS & PROJECTS FROM PRECUTS OR STASH*

Finished quilt size: 51" x 58½"
Finished block size: 4" x 8"
Finished connecting block size: 2" x 8"

Materials

Note: I used a precut 10" stack of Island Batik Blue Moon fabrics. For a scrappier look, use more than the number of fabric squares given.

- 13 or more 10" squares of assorted light and medium blue fabric
- 5 or more 10" squares of assorted dark blue fabric
- ⅝ yard gray crackle print fabric
- 2⅛ yards white tonal fabric
- ½ yard light blue fabric
- 56" x 65" backing fabric
- 56" x 65" batting
- WOF = width of fabric

Sew with ¼" seam allowance unless otherwise noted.

Cut the Fabrics

From assorted light and medium blue 10" squares, cut:

- (11) 4½" x 8½" rectangles for Block A
- (26) 4½" squares for Block B

From assorted dark blue 10" squares, cut:

- (22) 2" x 4½" rectangles for Block C
- (42) 1½" x 2½" rectangles for Connecting Blocks
- (12) 1½" squares for Half-Connecting Blocks

Note: The featured quilt uses identical fabrics for Block C and Connecting Blocks to create a "connecting" effect.

From gray crackle print fabric, cut:

- (3) 2½" x WOF strips. From the strips, cut: (28) 2½" x 4½" rectangles for Block B
- (2) 4" x WOF strips. From the strips, cut: (46) 1½" x 4" rectangles for Connecting and Half-Connecting Blocks

From white tonal fabric, cut:

- (5) 4½" x WOF strips.
  From 2 strips, cut: (24) 2½" x 4½" rectangles for Block B
  From 3 strips, cut: (22) 2½" x 4½" rectangles for Block C and (11) 1½" x 4½" rectangles for Block C
- (4) 4" x WOF strips.
  From the strips, cut:
  (44) 2½" x 4" rectangles for Connecting Blocks and
  (40) 1½" x 4" rectangles for Connecting Blocks
- (1) 4" x WOF strip. From the strip, cut: (18) 1½" x 4" rectangles for Half-Connecting Blocks
- (7) 2" x WOF strips. Sew the strips together along the short ends to make one continuous strip.
  From the strip, cut:
  (5) 2" x 48½" sashing strips
- (6) 2" x WOF strips. Sew the strips together along the short ends to make one continuous strip.
  From the strip, cut:
  (2) 2" x 48½" top/bottom border strips
  (2) 2" x 59" side border strips
- From light blue fabric, cut:
  (6) 2¼" x WOF binding strips

Block Assembly

Block B

1 Sew a 2½" x 4½" white tonal rectangle to opposite sides of a 4½" light or medium blue square. Press to make a white/blue Block B. Make a total of 12 white/blue Block B.

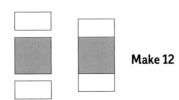

Make 12

2 In the same manner, sew a 2½" x 4½" gray crackle rectangle to opposite sides of a 4½" light or medium blue square. Press to make a gray/blue Block B. Make a total of 14 gray/blue Block B.

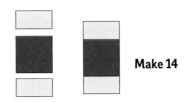

Make 14

Block C

1 Sew a 2" x 4½" dark blue rectangle to opposite sides of a 1½" x 4½" white tonal rectangle.

2 In the same manner, sew a 2½" x 4½" white tonal rectangle to the top and bottom of the sewn unit in step 1. Press to make a Block C. Make a total of 11 Block C.

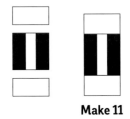

Make 11

Connecting Block D

Sew a 2½" x 4" white tonal rectangle to the opposite sides of a 1½" x 2½" dark blue rectangle to complete Connecting Block D. Make a total of 22 Connecting Block D.

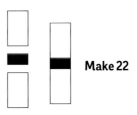

Make 22

Connecting Block E

Sew a 1½" x 4" white tonal rectangle and a 1½" x 4" gray crackle rectangle together along one long edge. Repeat to make 2 units. Sew the units to opposite sides of a 1½" x 2½" dark blue rectangle. Press to complete Connecting Block E. Make a total of 20 Connecting Block E.

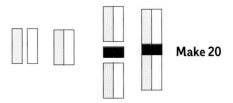

Make 20

Half-Connecting Blocks

1 Sew a 1½" x 4" gray crackle rectangle to opposite sides of a 1½" dark blue square. Press to complete a gray/blue Half-Connecting Block. Make a total of 3 gray/blue Half-Connecting Blocks.

Make 3

2 In the same manner, sew a 1½" x 4" white tonal rectangle to opposite sides of a 1½" dark blue square. Press to make a white/blue Half-Connecting Block. Make a total of 9 white/blue Half-Connecting Blocks.

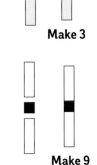

Make 9

Quilt Top Assembly

1 Referring to the Quilt Center Assembly Diagram, lay out the blocks, connecting blocks, half-connecting blocks, and the white tonal 2" x 48½" sashing strips in rows as shown.

2 Sew the pieces together in each row.

3 Sew a sashing strip to the top of rows 2 through 6.

4 Sew the rows together to complete the quilt center.

5 Sew a 2" x 48½" white tonal top/bottom border strip to the top and bottom of the quilt center.

6 Sew a 2" x 59" white tonal side border strip to opposite sides of the quilt center to complete the quilt top.

Finishing

1 Lay the backing fabric, wrong side up, on a flat surface. The backing fabric should be taut. Layer batting and quilt top, right side up, on top of backing to form a quilt sandwich. Baste the quilt sandwich.

2 Quilt as desired.

3 Sew the (6) 2¼" x WOF binding strips together along the short ends to make one continuous binding strip. Fold the piece in half lengthwise, wrong sides together, and press. Sew to the raw edge of the quilt top. Fold the binding over the raw edges and hand stitch in place on back of quilt.

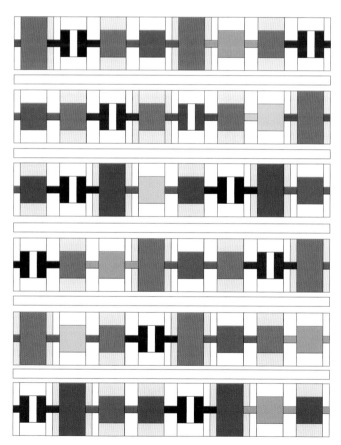

Quilt Top Assembly Diagram

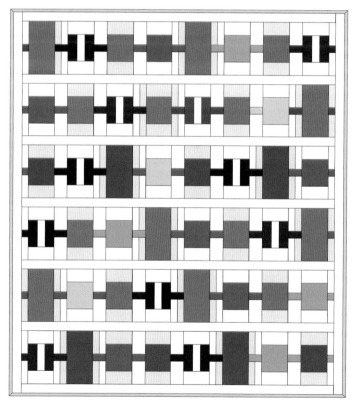

Care for a Cuppa? Wallhanging

BY WENDY SHEPPARD, FROM HER BOOK *CREATIVE NEW QUILTS & PROJECTS FROM PRECUTS OR STASH*

Finished block size: 6½"
Finished wallhanging size: 40" square

Materials

Note: I used a precut 10" layer cake and jelly roll bundle from Moda's Winterberry fabric line.

- ✛ (40) 10" squares assorted light to dark print fabric (separate the squares into light, medium, and dark groups)
- ✛ (4) 2½" x WOF assorted medium gray print fabric strips
- ✛ (4) 2½" x WOF assorted red print fabric strips
- ✛ (10–12) 2½" x WOF assorted light print fabric strips
- ✛ ½ yard light taupe polka dot fabric
- ✛ ¼ yard light fabric
- ✛ (5) 2½" x WOF binding strips
- ✛ 46" square backing fabric
- ✛ 46" square batting
- ✛ Layer Cake = 10" square
- ✛ Jelly Roll strip = 2½" x WOF
- ✛ WOF = width of fabric

Sew with ¼" seam allowance unless otherwise noted.

Cut the Fabrics

From light print 10" squares, cut:

- ✛ (9) 7" squares for appliqué block backgrounds

From medium to dark print 10" squares, cut:

- ✛ (22) 3" squares for inner border 2 appliqué shapes using the templates on page 55
  (9) cups
  (9) saucers
  (1) small steam
  (1) large steam
  (3) s
  (2) e
  (1) p
  (1) r
  (1) o

From assorted medium gray print strips, cut:

- ✛ (2) 2½" x 32½" inner border 3 strips
- ✛ (2) 2½" x 36½" inner border 3 strips

From assorted red print strips, cut:

- ✛ (2) 2½" x 36½" outer border strips
- ✛ (2) 2½" x 40½" outer border strips

From assorted light print strips, cut:

- ✛ (44) 1¼" x 3" inner border 2 rectangles
- ✛ (44) 1¼" x 4½" inner border 2 rectangles
- ✛ (1) 1½" x 4½" inner border 1 rectangle

From light taupe polka dot fabric, cut:

- ✛ (2) 1¾" x WOF strips.
  From the strips, cut:
  (6) 1¾" x 7" sashing rectangles
- ✛ (2) 1¾" x WOF strips.
  From the strips, cut:
  (2) 1¾" x 22½" sashing strips
- ✛ (4) 1½" x WOF strips.
  From the strips, cut:
  (2) 1½" x 22½" side inner border 1 strips
  (1) 1½" x 24½" bottom inner border 1 strip
  (1) 1½" x 18½" top inner border 1 strip
  (1) 1½" x 2½" top inner border 1 rectangle

From light fabric, cut:

- ✛ (2) 4½" x 12½" inner border 2 rectangle

Appliqué Block Assembly

Prepare the appliqué shapes using your favorite method. Fusible appliqué was used on the wallhanging. Referring to the diagram and the photo on page 55, arrange the cup and saucer appliqué pieces on the 7" background blocks. Sew the pieces in place using a favorite appliqué stitch. Make 9 appliqué blocks.

Wallhanging Center Assembly

1 Lay out 3 appliqué blocks and (2) 1¾" x 7" light taupe polka dot sashing rectangles in a row. Sew the pieces together to make a row. Make a total of 3 block rows.

2 Lay out the 3 block rows and 1¾" x 22½" light taupe polka dot sashing strips. Sew the pieces together to complete the wallhanging center.

Border Assembly

1 Sew 1½" x 22½" light taupe polka dot side inner border 1 strips to opposite sides of the wallhanging center. Sew the 1½" x 24½" light taupe polka dot bottom inner border 1 strip to the bottom of the wallhanging center.

2 Sew the 1½" x 18½" light taupe polka dot top inner border 1 rectangle, 1½" x 4½" light top inner border 1 rectangle and 1½" x 2½" light taupe polka dot top inner border 1 rectangle together to make a top inner border 1 strip. Sew the strip to the top of wallhanging center.

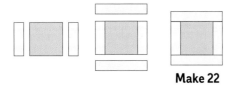

3 Sew 1¼" x 3" light inner border 2 rectangles to opposite sides of a 3" medium to dark print square. Sew 1¼" x 4½" light inner border 2 rectangles to the remaining sides of the square to complete a unit. Make a total of 22 units.

Make 22

4 Sew 6 units together in a row. Sew the row to the left side of the wallhanging center.

5 Sew 3 units and a 4½" x 12½" light inner border 2 rectangle into a row. Sew the row to the right side of the wallhanging center.

6 Sew 8 units together in a row. Sew the row to the bottom of the wallhanging center.

7 Sew 5 units and a 4½" x 12½" light inner border 2 rectangle into a row. Sew the row to the top of the wallhanging center.

8 Sew 2½" x 32½" gray inner border 3 strips to opposite sides of the wallhanging center. Sew 2½" x 36½" gray inner border 3 strips to the remaining sides of the wallhanging center.

9 Sew 2½" x 36½" red inner border 4 strips to opposite sides of the wallhanging center. Sew 2½" x 40½" red inner border 4 strips to the remaining sides of the wallhanging center to complete the wallhanging top.

10 Prepare the appliqué steam and letter shapes using your favorite method. Fusible appliqué was used on the wallhanging. Referring to the photo on page 55, arrange the appliqué pieces on the top right of border 2. Sew the pieces in place using a favorite appliqué stitch.

Finishing

1. Lay the backing fabric, wrong side up, on a flat surface. The backing fabric should be taut. Layer batting and quilt top, right side up, on top of backing to form a quilt sandwich. Baste the quilt sandwich.

2. Quilt as desired.

   Quilting notes: Appliqué blocks are quilted with background McTavishing motif; border is quilted with informal feathers in contrasting colors.

3. Sew the (5) 2½" x WOF binding strips together along the short ends to make one continuous binding strip. Fold the piece in half lengthwise, wrong sides together, and press. Sew to the raw edge of the quilt top. Fold the binding over the raw edges and hand stitch in place on back of quilt.

Templates

Large Steam Template

Small Steam Template

ENLARGE TEMPLATES
125%

Cup Template

Saucer Template

Templates have been reversed for fusible appliqué

Sliding Scale Baby Quilt

BY McB McMANUS AND E.B. UPDEGRAFF, FROM THEIR BOOK *EASY-CUT BABY QUILTS*

Cut the Fabrics

From gray solid fabric, cut:
+ (25) 2½" x WOF strips From the strips, cut:
    (20) 2½" x 8" rectangles
    (20) 2½" x 15" rectangles
    (20) 2½" x 23" rectangles

From binding fabric, cut:
+ (8) 2½" x WOF strips

Panel Assembly

1 Separate the assorted 2½" x WOF print strips into 10 sets of 4 strips each.

2 Sew a 2½" x 23" gray solid rectangle to one end of a print strip. Press the seams toward the gray strip to make an A strip set. Make 2 A strip sets.

Make 2 A

3 Sew a 2½" x 8" gray solid rectangle to one end of a print strip. Sew a 2½" x 15" rectangle to the opposite end of the print strip. Press seams toward the gray strips to make a B strip set. Make 2 B strip sets.

Make 2 B

4 Sew an A and B strip together along one long edge as shown. Press seams open to make a strip pair. Make 2 strip pairs.

Make 2 pairs

5 Sew strip pairs together as shown. Press seam open to make a strip panel. Make a total of 10 strip panels.

Make 10 panels

Quilt Assembly

1 Referring to the Quilt Assembly Diagram, lay out the strip panels as shown.

2 Sew the strip panels together. Alternate the sewing direction with each panel. This will prevent the strip panels from becoming wavy while sewing. Press seams open.

3 Carefully trim the side edges to square up the quilt top.

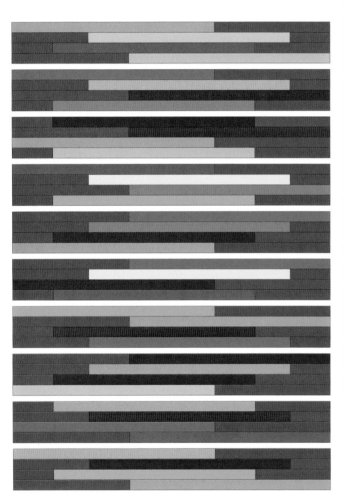

Quilt Assembly Diagram

Size Twist

Nap Bag: Referring to the bottom left image, sew 5 strip panels together. After layering, quilting, and binding, fold the quilt in half lengthwise with right sides together. Sew the bottom of the folded quilt together. Measure the long open edge and cut a sew-on Velcro® strip to fit the opening. Sew the Velcro® strip in place.

Approximate size: 31" x 40"

Finishing

1 Layer the backing, batting, and quilt top. Baste the layers together and hand or machine quilt as desired.

2 Sew the 2½"-wide binding strips together to make one continuous strip. Press the strip in half lengthwise, wrong sides together. Sew the binding to the front of the quilt, aligning the raw edges. Turn the binding over the edge to the back of the quilt and hand or machine stitch in place.

Easy-Cut Baby Quilts
#739 | $14.95

This book focuses on colorful, fun and easy projects that say "baby." Easy-going precuts and panels enable you to make the quilts in a weekend. Available at your favorite supplies store or bookstore. See page 96 or call 800-457-9112.

Color Block Baby Quilt

BY MCB MCMANUS AND E.B. UPDEGRAFF, FROM THEIR BOOK *EASY-CUT BABY QUILTS*

Finished quilt size: 53" x 59"

Materials

Note: half-yard cut = 18" x WOF

- ✛ (7) half-yard cuts in assorted prints
- ✛ ½ yard light solid fabric
- ✛ 3½ yards backing fabric
- ✛ ½ yard binding fabric
- ✛ 59" x 65" batting
- ✛ WOF = width of fabric Fabric quantities based on 42"- to 44"-wide, 100% cotton fabrics

Cut the Fabrics

From assorted prints, cut a total of:
- ✛ (3) 18" x 20" rectangles
- ✛ (4) 15½" x 22" rectangles
- ✛ From remaining fabric, cut: (19) 5" squares

From light solid fabric, cut:
- ✛ (3) 5" x WOF strips
  From the strips, cut: (20) 5" squares

From binding fabric, cut:
- ✛ (6) 2½" x WOF strips

Section Assembly

1 Sew the 18" x 20" rectangles together along the short edges to make the left quilt section. Press seams open.

2 Sew the 15½" x 22" rectangles together along the long edges to make the right quilt section. Press seams open.

3 Sew a light solid 5" square to opposite sides of a print 5" square. Press seams open to make an A segment. Make a total of 7 A segments.

Make 7 A segments

4 Sew a print 5" square to opposite sides of a light solid 5" square. Press seams open to make a B segment. Make a total of 6 B segments.

Make 6 B segments

5 Sew the A and B segments together, alternating the segments beginning with an A segment. Press seams open to make the center quilt section.

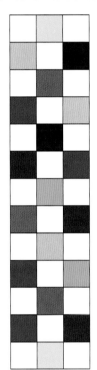

Quilt Assembly

1 Referring to the Quilt Assembly Diagram below, lay out the left, center, and right quilt sections.

2 Sew the left quilt section to the center quilt section. Press seams open.

3 Sew the right quilt section to the opposite side of the center quilt section. Press seams open to complete the quilt top.

Finishing

1 Square up the quilt top edges.

2 Layer the backing, batting, and quilt top. Baste the layers together and hand or machine quilt as desired.

3 Sew the 2½"-wide binding strips together to make one continuous strip. Press the strip in half lengthwise, wrong sides together. Sew the binding to the front of the quilt, aligning the raw edges. Turn the binding over the edge to the back of the quilt and hand or machine stitch in place.

Quilt Assembly Diagram

Fabric Blocks

1 For each block, sew together four 5" fabric squares as shown in Diagram A, starting and stopping ¼" from the top and bottom edges and backstitching to secure the seam. Press seam allowances open.

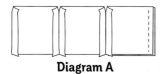

Diagram A

2 Sew together the remaining side edges of the first and fourth squares, starting and stopping ¼" from the top and bottom edges.

3 Sew a 5" fabric square to the top edge of the block sides as shown in Diagram B. To make a sharp turn at the corners, leave the needle down in the fabric, lift the presser foot, and turn the fabric.

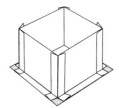

Diagram B

4 Sew a second square to the bottom edge of the block sides in the same manner, leaving one edge open for turning. Trim each corner as shown in Diagram C.

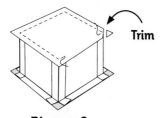

Trim

Diagram C

5 Turn the fabric block right side out. Tuck a foam cube into the fabric block through the opening. Whipstitch the opening closed.

Color Fusion Quilt

BY JEAN ANN WRIGHT, FROM HER BOOK *JELLY ROLL JAZZ*

Jazz fusion was developed during the 1970s and 1980s. It is a musical genre that mixes jazz with rock and blues rhythms. Fusion allowed jazz musicians to blend the popularity of rock music with jazz and appeal to a larger listening audience.

Finished quilt size: 58" x 62"

Design Roll bundle = 2½" x WOF strips
WOF = Width of fabric

Note: Sew with a ¼" seam allowance

Materials

+ 1 design roll bundle of (20) 2½" x WOF strips
+ 1½ yards white fabric
+ 1 yard gray fabric
+ 3½ yards backing fabric
+ Twin-size batting

Cut the Fabrics

Separate the precut strips into 2 gray print strips and 18 color print strips.

From 1 gray print strip, cut:

+ (4) 2½" x 6½" rectangles for spacers

From 1 gray print strip, cut:

+ (13) 2½" squares for spacers

From each (18) color print strip, cut:

+ (4) 2½" x 8½" rectangles for blocks
+ (1) 2½" square for blocks.

From white fabric, cut:

+ (3) 4½" x WOF strips. From the strips, cut: (8) 4½" x 6½" rectangles for spacers, (26) 2½" x 4½" rectangles for spacers
+ (9) 2½" x WOF strips. From the strips, cut: (72) 2½" x 4½" rectangles for blocks
+ (6) 4½" x WOF strips. Sew the strips together end-to-end and cut: (2) 4½" x 58½" top/bottom outer border strips, (2) 4½" x 50½" side outer border strips

From gray fabric, cut:

+ (6) 2½" x WOF strips. Sew the strips together end-to-end and cut: (2) 2½" x 44¾" top/bottom inner border strips, (2) 2½" x 52½" side inner border strips
+ (6) 2¼" x WOF binding strips

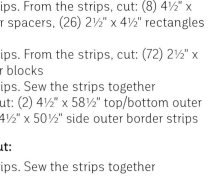

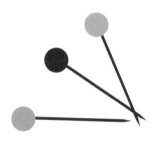

Block and Spacer Assembly

1   Separate (4) 2½" x 8½" matching color print rectangles, (1) 2½" contrasting color print square, and (4) 2½" x 4½" white rectangles into a group. This group will make 1 block. Separate pieces into 18 groups.

2   Lay a 2½" color print square on a 2½" x 4½" white rectangle, right sides together. Referring to the illustration, stitch a partial seam approximately 1¾" long.

3   Fold the square out and press seams toward the square to make unit A.

Unit A

4   Lay a 2½" x 4½" white rectangle on the adjacent side of unit A. Stitch the pieces together as shown. Press rectangle open to make unit B.

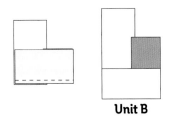

Unit B

5   Sew a 2½" x 4½" white rectangle to unit B as shown. Press rectangle open to make unit C.

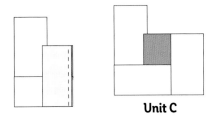

Unit C

6   Sew a 2½" x 4½" white rectangle to the remaining side of unit C, taking care to fold the first rectangle away from the square as you stitch. (You do not want to catch it in the seam.) Press rectangle open.

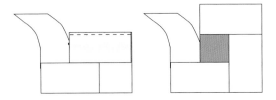

7   Fold the first rectangle over the square and the last rectangle you added. Finish sewing the partial seam to complete the block center. Press.

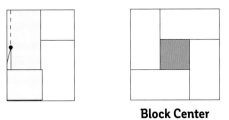

Block Center

8   In the same manner, sew the (4) 2½" x 8½" matching color print strips around the block center to complete the block. Make a total of 18 blocks.

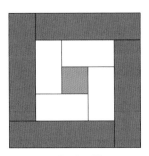

Make 18

9   Sew 2½" x 4½" white rectangles to opposite sides of a 2½" gray print square to make a narrow spacer. Make 13 narrow spacers.

10 Sew 4½" x 6½" white rectangles to opposite sides of a 2½" x 6½" gray print strip to make a wide spacer unit. Make 4 wide spacers.

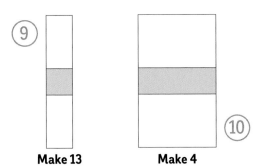

Make 13   **Make 4**

Quilt Assembly

1. Referring to the Quilt Assembly Diagram, lay out the blocks, narrow and wide spacers in 5 horizontal rows.

2. Sew the pieces together in rows. Sew the rows together to complete the quilt center. Press seams as each row is added.

Adding the Borders

1. Sew the 2½" x 44¾" gray top/bottom inner border strips to the top and bottom of the quilt top. Sew the 2½" x 52½" gray side inner border strips to opposite sides of the quilt top. Press seams toward borders.

2. Sew the 4½" x 58½" white side outer border strips to the top and bottom of the quilt top. Sew the 4½" x 50½" white top/bottom outer border strips to opposite sides of the quilt top. Press seams toward borders to compete the quilt top.

Finishing

1. Layer the quilt top, batting, and backing.

2. Baste the layers together. Hand or machine quilt as desired. The featured quilt was quilted using gently curving lines that complemented the classic designs in the design roll.

3. Sew the (6) 2¼" x WOF binding strips together along the short edges to make one continuous binding strip. Press seams open.

4. Press the strip in half lengthwise, wrong sides together, and sew to the raw edge of the quilt top. Fold binding over raw edges and hand stitch in place.

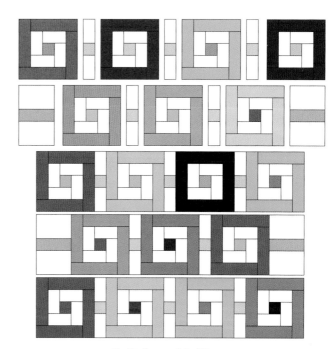

Quilt Assembly Diagram

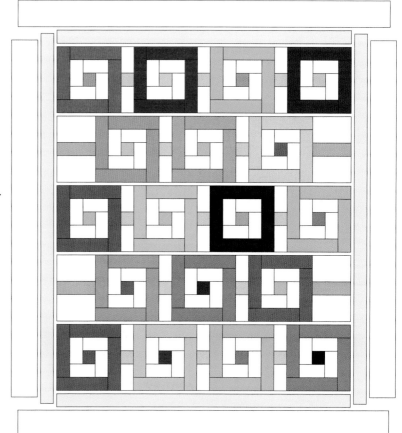

Pick Up Sticks Quilt

BY JEAN ANN WRIGHT, FROM HER BOOK *JELLY ROLL JAZZ*

A jazz drummer is influenced by many individual drummers and the styles that reflect where they have lived, whether New Orleans, the Caribbean, or Africa. A gradual "freeing" of the beat has emerged over time. The 16 blocks in this quilt has a series of "sticks" or strips around the center square that are randomly trimmed so no two strips are exactly the same size or shape.

Finished quilt size: 48" x 48"

Precut bundle = 2½" x WOF strips
WOF = Width of fabric

Note: Sew with a ¼" seam allowance

Materials

- ✛ 1 precut bundle of (40) 2½" x WOF strips
- ✛ ¼ yard gray small dot fabric
- ✛ ⅛ yard gray large dot fabric
- ✛ 1 yard gray fabric
- ✛ 3 yards backing fabric
- ✛ Twin-size batting

Cut the Fabrics

Separate the precut strips into light and dark color groups. The strips will be cut the length needed when making the blocks.

From gray small dot fabric, cut:

- ✛ (2) 3½" x WOF strips From the strips, cut:
  (16) 3½" center squares

From gray large dot fabric, cut:

- ✛ (4) 4½" squares for cornerstones

From gray fabric, cut:

- ✛ (4) 4½" x 40½" border strips
- ✛ (5) 2¼" x WOF binding strips

Block Assembly

Precut strips are sewn around a center square and trimmed at random angles to create the block.

1 Sew a 2½" light precut strip to one side of a 3½" gray small dot center square. Trim the strip approximately 1" longer than the center square.

2 Sew another light precut strip to the center square overlapping the first strip and extending approximately 1" past the end of the strip.

3 In the same manner, sew dark precut strips to the remaining sides of the center square.

4 Trim the unit to 5½" square using a ruler and rotary cutter. Position the ruler at random angles when cutting.

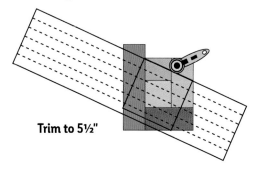

Trim to 5½"

5 Repeat steps 1-3 to sew an additional four precut strips around the center square. Trim the unit to 8" square.

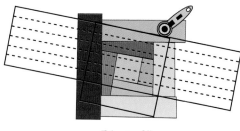

Trim to 8"

6 Repeat steps 1-3 to sew an additional four precut strips around the center square. Trim the unit to 10½" square to complete a block. Make a total of 16 blocks.

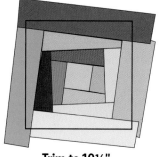

Trim to 10½"

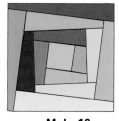

Make 16

Quilt Center Assembly

1 Sew the blocks together in sets of four. The two dark sides in each block should be positioned on the outer edges with the light sides meeting in the center of the set. Make a total of four block sets.

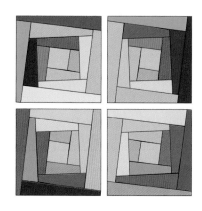

Make 4

2 Referring to the Quilt Center Assembly Diagram, lay out the four block sets. Sew the sets together to complete the quilt center.

Adding the Borders

1. Sew a 4½" x 40½" gray border strip to opposite sides of the quilt center. Press seams toward borders.

2. Sew a 4½" gray large dot cornerstone to opposite short edges of the remaining border strips to complete top/bottom borders.

3. Sew the top/bottom borders to the top and bottom of the quilt center to complete the quilt top.

Finishing

1. Layer the quilt top, batting, and backing.

2. Baste the layers together. Hand or machine quilt as desired. The featured quilt was quilted using a series of long, straight stitching in irregular widths from top to bottom.

3. Sew (5) 2¼" x WOF binding strips together along the short edges to make one continuous binding strip. Press seams open.

4. Press the strip in half lengthwise, wrong sides together, and sew to the raw edge of the quilt top. Fold binding over raw edges and hand stitch in place.

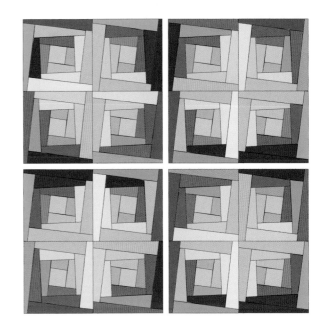

Quilt Center Assembly Diagram

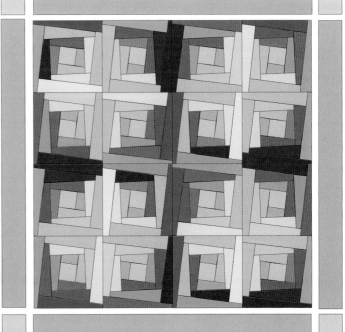

Carnival Confetti Quilt

BY JEAN ANN WRIGHT, FROM HER BOOK *JELLY ROLL JAMBALAYA QUILTS*

What would a carnival like Mardi Gras be without confetti? I made my Carnival Confetti Quilt using squares, but many different widths of fabric strips can be used to produce intricate patterns.

Finished quilt size: 55" x 70"

Jelly Roll strip = 2½" x WOF
WOF = Width of fabric
LOF = Length of fabric

Note: Sew with a ¼" seam allowance

Materials

- 1 Jelly Roll bundle containing 40 strips
- 2¼ yards white fabric
- 4¼ yards backing fabric
- Twin-size batting

Cut the Fabrics

Note: Separate the jelly roll bundle into 30 bright strips and 10 light or white strips.

From 20 bright jelly roll strips, cut:

- Each strip into (4) 2½" x 10" rectangles for a total of 80 rectangles

From 7 light or white jelly roll strips, cut:

- Each strip into (4) 2½" x 10" rectangles for a total of 28 rectangles.
- From 1 light or white jelly roll strip, cut:
  (2) 2½" x 10" rectangles and (2) 2½" x 7½" rectangles. Cut the remaining portion of the strip into 2½" squares

Block Assembly

1 Choose (5) 2½" x 10" bright rectangles and (2) 2½" x 10" light rectangles. Sew the rectangles together with a light rectangle on each outside edge as shown. Press to make a strip set. Make 15 strip sets.

2 Cut each strip set into (4) 2½" segments for a total of 60 segments.

Make 15

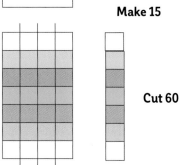

Cut 60

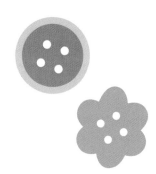

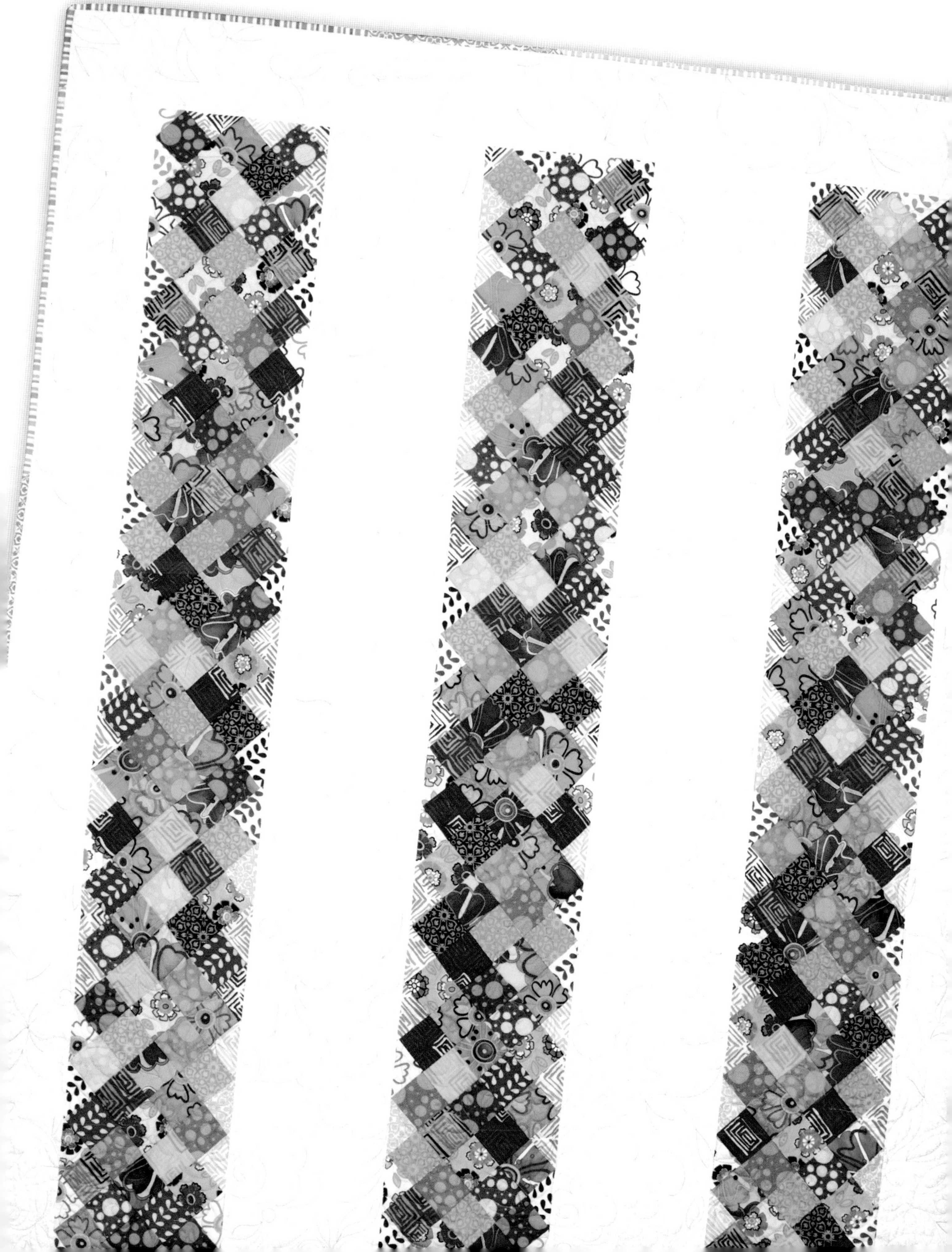

3 From 4 bright jelly roll strips, cut each strip into (5) 2½" x 7½" rectangles for a total of 20 rectangles. You will use 18 of these rectangles for end strip units.

4 From 2 light or white jelly roll strips, cut a total of (10) 2½" x 7½" rectangles.

5 Choose (3) 2½" x 7½" bright rectangles and (2) 2½" x 7½" light rectangles. Sew the rectangles together with a light rectangle on each outside edge as shown. Press to make an end unit strip set. Make 2 end unit strip sets. Carefully cut the strip sets into (6) 2½" end units.

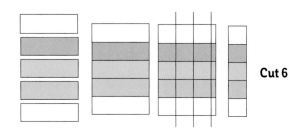

Cut 6

6 From a remaining bright jelly roll strip, cut (6) 2½" squares. Cut any remaining portions of the light strips into 2½" squares.

7 Sew light 2½" squares to opposite sides of a bright 2½" square. Sew an additional light 2½" square to one side as shown to make a corner end unit. Make 6 corner end units.

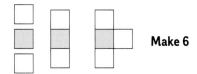

Make 6

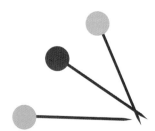

Quilt Assembly

1 Separate the strip sets into three random color groups of (20) 2½" x 10" strips.

2 Sew the strips sets together, offsetting each row by one square as shown.

3 Referring to the Row Assembly Diagram, sew an end unit strip to opposite ends of each row. Sew a corner end unit to opposite ends of each row.

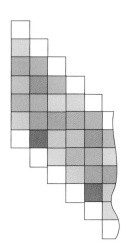

4 Using a rotary cutter and ruler, square up the sides and ends of each pieced row as shown. Take care to allow a ¼" seam allowance on all sides.

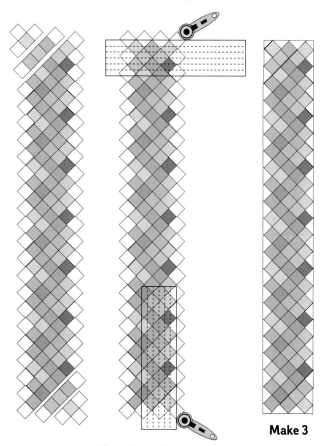

Make 3

Row Assembly Diagram

5 Measure a pieced row vertically from top to bottom. The measurement should be approximately 57" to 58" long. From the white fabric, cut (2) 8½" x length of the row measurement rows. Sew the 3 pieced rows and 2 white rows together to complete the quilt center.

6 From the white fabric, cut (2) 6½" x length of the row determined in step 5 side borders. Sew the side borders to opposite sides of the quilt center.

7 Fold the quilt in half, top to bottom, before measuring the width. Measure the quilt from side to side at the fold line to determine its width. The measurement should be approximately 55". From the white fabric, cut (2) 6½" x width of the quilt top/bottom border strips. Sew these borders to the top and bottom of the quilt center to complete the quilt top.

Finishing

1 Layer the quilt top, batting, and backing. Baste the layers together. Hand or machine quilt as desired.

2 Sew the remaining bright jelly roll strips together end-to-end to make one continuous binding strip. Fold the strip in half lengthwise with wrong sides together and press. Bind the quilt edges to finish.

Quilt Assembly Diagram

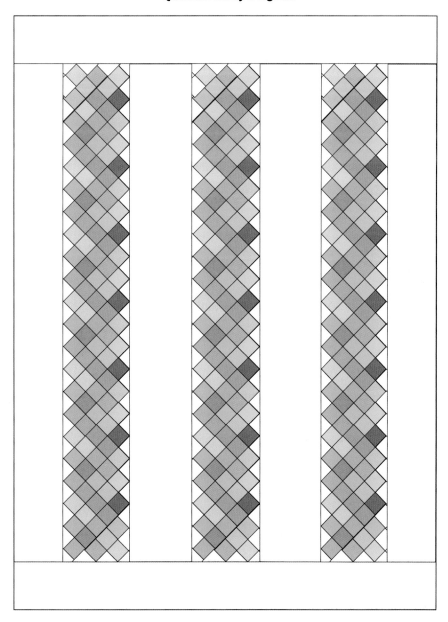

Mardi Gras Throws Quilt

BY JEAN ANN WRIGHT, FROM HER BOOK *JELLY ROLL JAMBALAYA QUILTS*

Modern prints in bright colors make a bold statement—perfect for sewing rows of hexagon Mardi Gras throws. What are throws? Beads, of course, strings and strings of beads. During Mardi Gras, these inexpensive trinkets are tossed from parade floats in response to cries from the spectators yelling, "Throw me something, throw me something!"

Finished quilt size: 56" x 66"

Jelly Roll strip = 2½" x WOF
WOF = Width of fabric
LOF = Length of fabric

Note: Sew with a ¼" seam allowance

Materials

✢ 1 Jelly Roll bundle

Note: You will use 39 of the (40) 2½" strips

✢ 2 yards triangle and border fabric
✢ ⅔ yard contrasting binding fabric
✢ 4 yards backing fabric
✢ Twin-size batting
✢ (65) 6⅞" x 6" Blocks

Block Assembly

1 Sew 3 Jelly Roll strips together along the long edges as shown. Press the seams open to make a strip set. Make 13 strip sets.

Make 13

2 Use the hexagon template on page 79 to cut 5 hexagons from each strip set. Cut a total of 65 hexagons from the strip sets.

Cut 65

3 Using the remaining pieces of strip sets from step 2, cut 10 partial hexagons using the template on page 79.

Cut 10

4 From the triangle fabric, cut (11) 3¾" x width of fabric strips. Use the triangle template on page 79 or refer to Cutting 60-Degree Triangles on page 81 to cut triangles from each strip. Cut a total of 150 triangles.

Cut 150

5 Sew a triangle to opposite sides of a hexagon as shown to make a hexagon block. Make 65 hexagon blocks.

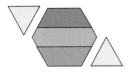 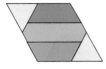

Make 65

6 Sew a triangle to one side of a partial hexagon as shown to make a partial hexagon block. Make 10 partial hexagon blocks.

Make 10

Quilt Assembly

1 Referring to the Quilt Assembly diagram below right, lay out the partial hexagon blocks, the hexagon blocks, and the triangles in 10 rows as shown.

Note: The odd numbered rows begin and end with a partial hexagon block, and the even numbered rows begin and end with a hexagon block and triangles.

2 Sew the pieces together in rows. Sew the rows together, matching the seams of the triangles and hexagons.

3 Using a rotary cutter and ruler, cut the ends of the rows so the partial hexagon blocks and triangles are trimmed in an even line to complete the quilt center.

4 From the border fabric, cut (6) 4½" x WOF strips. Sew the strips together end-to-end to form a continuous strip. From the strip, cut (2) 4½" x 55½" strips for the top and bottom borders and (2) 4½" x 59" strips for the side borders. Sew the side borders to opposite sides of the quilt center. Sew the top and bottom borders to the top and bottom of the quilt center to complete the quilt top.

Finishing

1 Layer the quilt top, batting, and backing. Baste the layers together. Hand or machine quilt as desired.

2 From the contrasting binding fabric, cut (7) 2¼" x LOF binding strips. Sew the strips together end-to-end to make one continuous binding strip. Fold the strip in half lengthwise with wrong sides together and press. Bind the quilt edges to finish.

Trim line   **Trim line**

Quilt Assembly Diagram

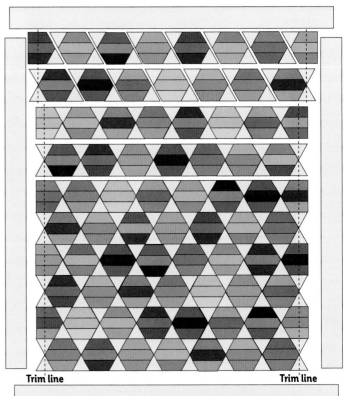

Trim line   **Trim line**

Templates

ENLARGE TEMPLATES
125%

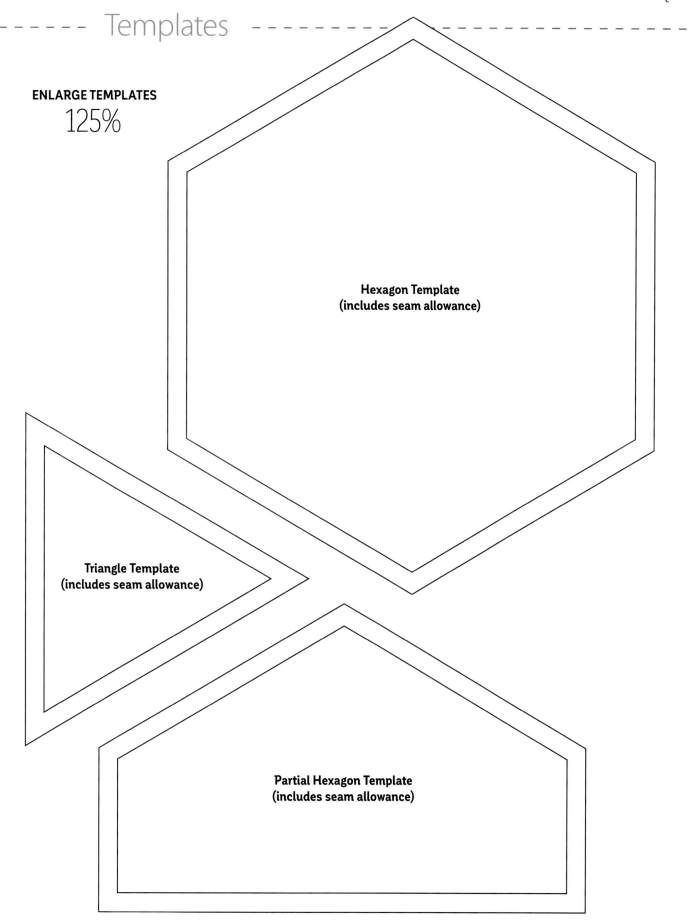

Hexagon Template
(includes seam allowance)

Triangle Template
(includes seam allowance)

Partial Hexagon Template
(includes seam allowance)

Cutting Hexagons and 60-degree Triangles

Modern quilters are rediscovering the hexagon shape and its many possibilities for creative design. While many templates are available for cutting perfect hexagons, they can also be cut using a standard quilter's ruler. These rulers are marked with 45- and 60-degree angles for cutting triangles and other angled shapes. The hexagon is made using the 60-degree mark.

Cutting Hexagons

1 Sew 3 jelly roll strips together along the long edges to create a strip set. Press the seams open to reduce bulk when cutting. Cut the strip set into (5) 7½" segments. The hexagons will be cut from these segments. Finger-press each segment in half lengthwise.

Tip: Use spray starch to add body to the strip set.

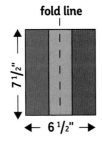

2 Position the 60-degree line on the ruler even with the long edge of the segment. Trim along this angle.

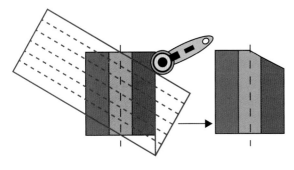

3 To trim the adjacent side of the hexagon, position the 60-degree line of the ruler on the angle cut in step 2. Trim along this angle.

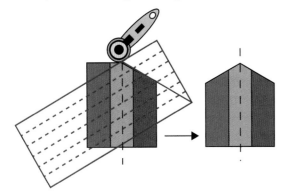

4 Turn the trimmed segment and position the 60-degree line of the ruler on the angle cut in step 3. Trim along this angle.

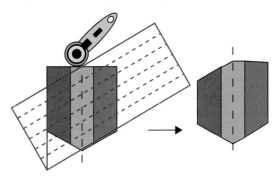

5 Reposition the ruler on the angle cut in step 2. Trim along the angle to complete the hexagon.

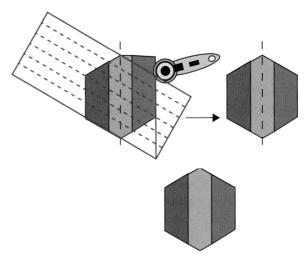

Cutting 60-Degree Triangles

1 Cut a 3¾" x WOF strip. Position the 60-degree line of the ruler on the top edge of the fabric strip as shown. Trim along the left angle of the ruler.

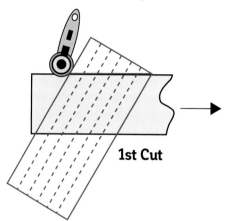

1st Cut

2 Reposition the 60-degree line of the ruler on the angle cut in step 1 as shown. The tip of the ruler should be even with the top of the fabric strip. Cut along the right angle of the ruler to make a triangle.

Note: To make multiple triangles, turn the ruler and align the 60-degree ruler line with the previous cut angle.

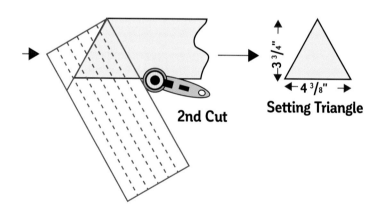

2nd Cut

$3\,^{3}/_{4}$"

$4\,^{3}/_{8}$"

Setting Triangle

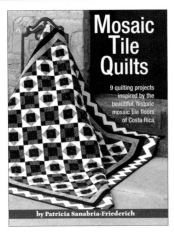

Mosaic Tile Quilts
$22.95 • #463

Best of Circle of Nine
$24.95 • #692

**Creative New Quilts & Projects
from Precuts or Stash**
$21.95 • #753C

Easy-Cut Baby Quilts
$14.95 • #739

**Fast-Fold Hexies from
Pre-cuts & Stash**
$12.95 • #951F

Jelly Roll Jazz
$14.95 • #838

Jelly Roll Jambalaya Quilts
$14.95 • #494

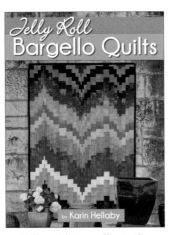

Jelly Roll Bargello Quilts
$18.95 • #010

Mini Wonderful Curves
$22.95 • #999

By Phone: 800-457-9112 • **Direct:** 717-560-4703
Fax: 717-560-4702
Online at: www.FoxChapelPublishing.com
By Mail: Send Check or Money Order to
Fox Chapel Publishing
903 Square St.
Mount Joy, PA 17552

DESIGN ORIGINALS

Fast-Fold Hexies

QUILTING PROJECTS

A few years ago, Mary M. Hogan figured out how to make hexie units by folding hexagons from circles, inserting batting, and then adding another small hexagon on top to cover the raw edges. Using this technique creates a small complete hexie unit. Sewing hexie units together makes a two-sided quilt with no separate batting, backing, or binding!

Fast-Fold Hexies Tools & Techniques

BY MARY M. HOGAN, FROM HER BOOK *FAST-FOLD HEXIES FROM PRE-CUTS & STASH*

The Fast-Fold Hexie technique uses circles of fabric and hexagonal pieces of batting to make quilt-as-you-go hexie units. When sewing by machine, a project comes together quickly. However, you may choose to sew your hexies by hand which will make your project portable.

Fabric

For best results, use quality quilting fabric in two or more contrasting colors. This is a great opportunity to use precuts. The templates in this article make it possible to use 2½" precut squares, 2½" strips, and 5" and 10" squares. If you are cutting a lot of circles, cut 5" or 10" by width of fabric strips. And, remember, small pieces in your stash will create a very scrappy look.

This article focuses on using precut fabric sizes for your fast-fold hexies; however, you can use any size circle. The hexagon batting should be half the size of the circle (if you use a 12" circle, use a 6" hexagon).

Work surface

You need a work surface you can stick pins into as you fold the hexagon shapes. A thick piece of corrugated cardboard or foam core will work well. I use an empty fabric bolt as my pinnable work surface.

Batting

If your project is small, use scraps of batting. Specific batting requirements are given for each project.

Other supplies

÷ Long straight pins
÷ Scissors
÷ Pencil or pen for tracing templates
÷ Template material such as paper or cardstock

If you plan to join hexagons by hand:

÷ Hand-sewing needles
÷ Thimble and thread

Making a Fast-Fold Hexie Unit

Prepare the templates, using paper for circle templates and cardstock for hexagon shapes.

For a large hexagon, trace:
- ✛ 10" Circle Template
- ✛ 5" Circle Template
- ✛ Large Hexagon Template

For a small hexagon, trace:
- ✛ 5" Circle Template
- ✛ 2½" Circle Template
- ✛ Small Hexagon Template

TIP:

4 to 6 circles can be cut at one time; layer fabric and template and pin through all layers, cut. Batting can be cut with scissors, but no more than two at a time.

Folding the large hexagon

1 Using the 10" Circle, 5" Circle Templates, and Large Hexagon Template, cut two fabric circles and one batting hexagon. (In this step-by-step, a large hexagon is constructed.)

2 Orient the fabric circle so the lengthwise straight of grain runs vertically to keep hexagon from stretching after construction. To find the center of a 10" fabric circle, fold in half then in half again, finger-pressing each fold.

3 Place circle wrong side up on a pinnable work surface. Center batting hexagon on the circle as shown, matching points with the horizontal fold line on fabric. Place a pin through the center of batting, fabric, and work surface.

4 Fold over the top edge of circle, as shown, so the fold meets the pin at the center. Finger press the fold.

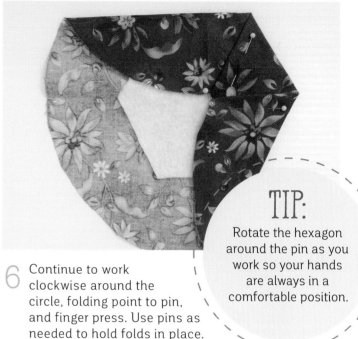

5 Working clockwise, fold right point created by the first fold to the pin at center and finger press.

6 Continue to work clockwise around the circle, folding point to pin, and finger press. Use pins as needed to hold folds in place.

TIP:
Rotate the hexagon around the pin as you work so your hands are always in a comfortable position.

7 After the fourth fold, make sure the first and fourth fold are parallel. If not, open and fold again or adjust the last fold slightly.

8 Before making the final fold, trim the curve as shown, so the raw edge will not show after making the final fold. Fold last point to the pin. This hexagon is referred to as the base hexagon. Set aside.

Folding the small hexagon

With the smaller fabric circle, find the center of the circle as you did in step 2. Place a pin through center and work surface. Fold the circle, referring to steps 3 to 7, without using a batting hexagon. This hexagon is referred to as the "topper."

Assembling a Hexie Unit

Sewing by machine

1 Place the large base hexagon on your work surface, folded side up. Center the small hexagon, or topper, folded side down on top of the base hexagon, centering the points of the topper between the folds of the base hexagon. Remove any pins in the base hexagon as you pin the small hexagon in place.

Note: The "envelope" is the section of the base hexagon between your first and last folds, as indicated by arrows in photo above. The folds face each other. When joining hexie units together, keeping all the envelopes oriented in the same direction will maintain your straight of grain.

2 Sew the topper in place, using a straight, buttonhole, zigzag, or decorative stitch. Stitch ⅜" from the outer edge of the base hexagon to complete your hexie unit. Stitching the topper down and sewing around the edge is the quilting that holds the layers together.

TIP:
Whether sewing by machine or by hand, always start and stop with very short locking stitches.

Sewing by hand

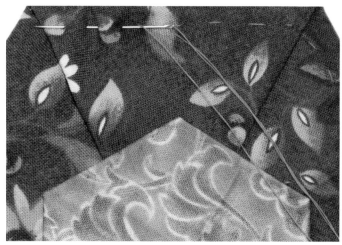

1 To sew the top hexagon by hand, sew a running stitch through all layers near the outside edge of the small hexagon, as shown.

2 Sew another round of running stitches through all layers ⅜" in from the edge of base hexagon.

Note: For hexie units made from a 5" circle base, stitch ¼" from the outside edge to complete your hexie unit.

Sewing Hexie Units Together

Sewing by machine

It's amazing how quickly a project can go together sewing with your machine. It's a chance to use different decorative or utility stitches that will cross over from one hexie unit to another. Experiment with stitches and size of stitch as well as variegated, contrasting, or matching threads. Since your thread choice is your "quilting" color, remember to think about the back of the quilt; your project is actually two-sided!

With right sides up, butt two hexie units together as shown. Using your selected stitch, pass hexagons through your machine, taking care that stitches span the edges of both hexie units.

TIP:

If needed, use a pin to help hold hexie units together while sewing. Use a stiletto to help ease the edges of the hexagons if not quite the same length.

Sewing by hand

One of the things I love about sewing hexies by hand is that it makes a project completely portable. Throw your hexies in a bag along with needle, thread, and scissors, and take them along everywhere you go.

You can mix and match hand and machine stitching on your project — there are no rules, so use the method you prefer!

1 Place two hexie units right sides together. Using a single thread, bury a small knot at the beginning of your stitches. Make a few very small stitches to lock thread in place. Whipstitch along one side of the hexie units.

2 Sew to the end and take a few locking stitches and bury the thread.

Note: Contrasting thread is used here to show the stitches. You will want to use a threads that blends well with your fabric.

Assembling Your Projects

After you have completed the hexie units for your project, you can sew them together by hand or machine. When using a machine, consider assembly order and passing the bulk of the project through the throat of your machine as your project gets larger. Use the diagrams below to get started.

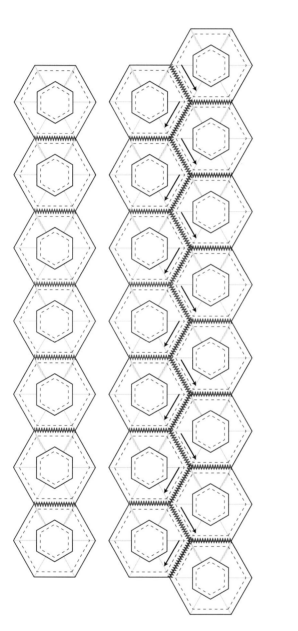

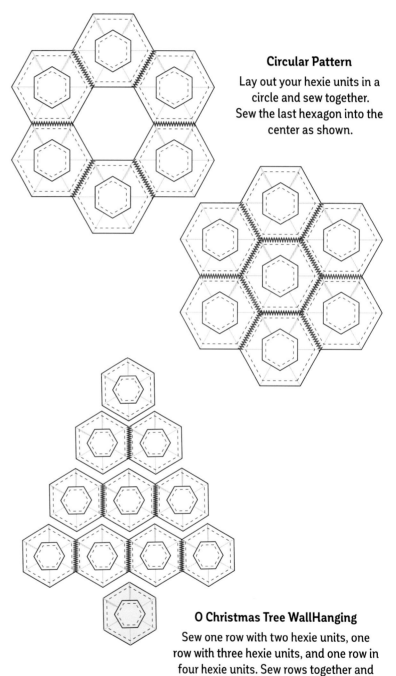

Circular Pattern

Lay out your hexie units in a circle and sew together. Sew the last hexagon into the center as shown.

Breaking Away Quilt

Sew hexie units into a column, then sew columns together, stitching in one direction as shown.

O Christmas Tree WallHanging

Sew one row with two hexie units, one row with three hexie units, and one row in four hexie units. Sew rows together and add top and bottom hexie units.

Breaking Away Quilt

BY MARY M. HOGAN, FROM HER BOOK *FAST-FOLD HEXIES FROM PRE-CUTS & STASH*

In this quilt, I wanted to suggest hexagons spreading out and escaping from the lower left. Exact placement of color and value is less important than giving the overall impression of movement away from the corner.

Finished size: 49" × 56" • 121 Hexie Units

Materials

Note: Fabric requirements are based on 42" wide fabric. WOF = width of fabric.

✤ (40) precut 10" print squares or 3 yards assorted fabric
✤ (81) precut 10" white squares or 6 yards white fabric
✤ (40) precut 5" print squares or 1 yard assorted fabrics
✤ (81) precut 5" white squares or 1¾ yards white fabric
✤ 2½ yards of batting (45" wide)
✤ 10" Circle Template
✤ 5" Circle Template
✤ Large Hexagon Template

Cut the Fabrics

From print fabric, cut:

✤ (40) 10" circles
✤ (40) 5" circles

From white fabric, cut:

✤ (81) 10" circles
✤ (81) 5" circles

From batting, cut:

✤ (121) hexagons using the Large Hexagon Template

Making the Hexie units

1 Using the 10" circles, fold (40) print base hexagons and (81) white base hexagons, referring to instructions on pages 84 to 87.

2 Construct 27 hexie units with white base hexagons and print toppers, 54 hexie units with white bases and white toppers, 27 hexie units with print bases and white toppers, and 13 hexie units with print bases and print toppers.

3 Stitch ⅜" from outer edge of large hexagon to add stability and quilting.

Quilt Assembly

This throw was made by joining the hexagons with a machine. If you prefer, you can join the hexagons by hand. See page 88 for tips on sewing the hexies by hand.

1 Arrange hexie units in a pleasing layout of 11 columns with 11 hexie units in each column. See the photo on page 89.

2 Referring to page 89, sew hexie units into columns, one on top of the other, with a joining stitch (utility zigzag or other decorative stitch).

3 Working from left to right, sew columns into pairs, leaving the last column separate. Join pairs to complete the quilt, adding the single column last. See page 89 for tips on sewing the column pairs together.

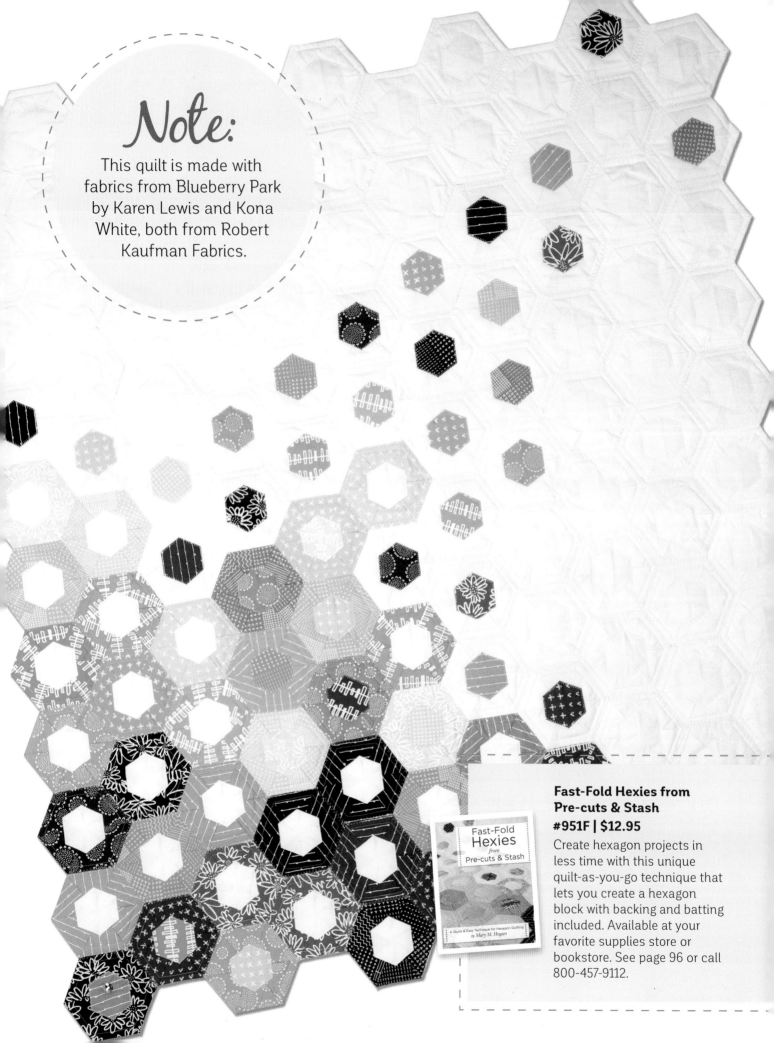

Note:

This quilt is made with fabrics from Blueberry Park by Karen Lewis and Kona White, both from Robert Kaufman Fabrics.

O Christmas Tree Wallhanging

BY MARY M. HOGAN, FROM HER BOOK *FAST-FOLD HEXIES FROM PRE-CUTS & STASH*

This project is made using the 5" circle, 2½" circle, and the Small Hexagon Template. For a larger wallhanging, use the larger templates and make 11 large hexie units.

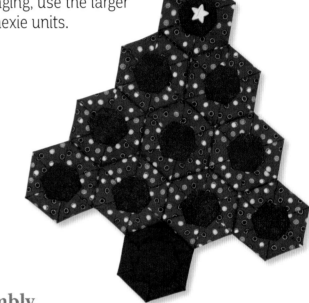

Finished size: 10" × 11" | 11 Hexie Units

Materials

Note: Fabric requirements are based on 42" wide fabric. WOF = width of fabric.

- ✧ (10) 5" precut squares or (1) fat quarter green dot fabric
- ✧ (10) 2½" precut squares or (1) fat eighth red fabric
- ✧ (1) 5" precut square or scrap brown fabric
- ✧ (1) 2½" square or scrap brown fabric
- ✧ ⅛ yard lightweight batting (45" wide)
- ✧ Star sew-on button
- ✧ 5" Circle Template
- ✧ 2½" Circle Template
- ✧ Small Hexagon Template

Cut the Fabrics

From green dot fabric, cut:
- ✧ (10) 5" circles

From red fabric, cut:
- ✧ (10) 2½" circles

From brown fabric, cut:
- ✧ (1) 5" circle
- ✧ (1) 2½" circle

From batting, cut:
- ✧ (11) hexagons using the Small Hexagon Template

Note: Consider adding embellishments to your Fast-Fold Hexie projects such as the star button and charms in the photo. Hand embroidery stitches, heat-set rhinestones, and contrasting or decorative threads are just a few ideas to try!

Assembly

1 Referring to instructions on pages 84 to 87, construct 10 hexie units with green dot bases and red toppers, and 1 hexie unit with brown base and brown topper.

2 Lay out hexagons as shown.

3 Referring to pages 88 to 89, sew hexagon units together into rows either by hand or machine.

4 Sew a star button onto the top hexagon to complete the wallhanging.

Hexie Templates

Large Hexagon Template

**Batting template for hexagon base unit
folded from a 10" circle**

Small Hexagon Template

**Batting template for hexagon base unit
folded from a 5" circle**

Visit:

*https://FoxChapelPublishing
.com/Landauer* for additional
projects and templates!

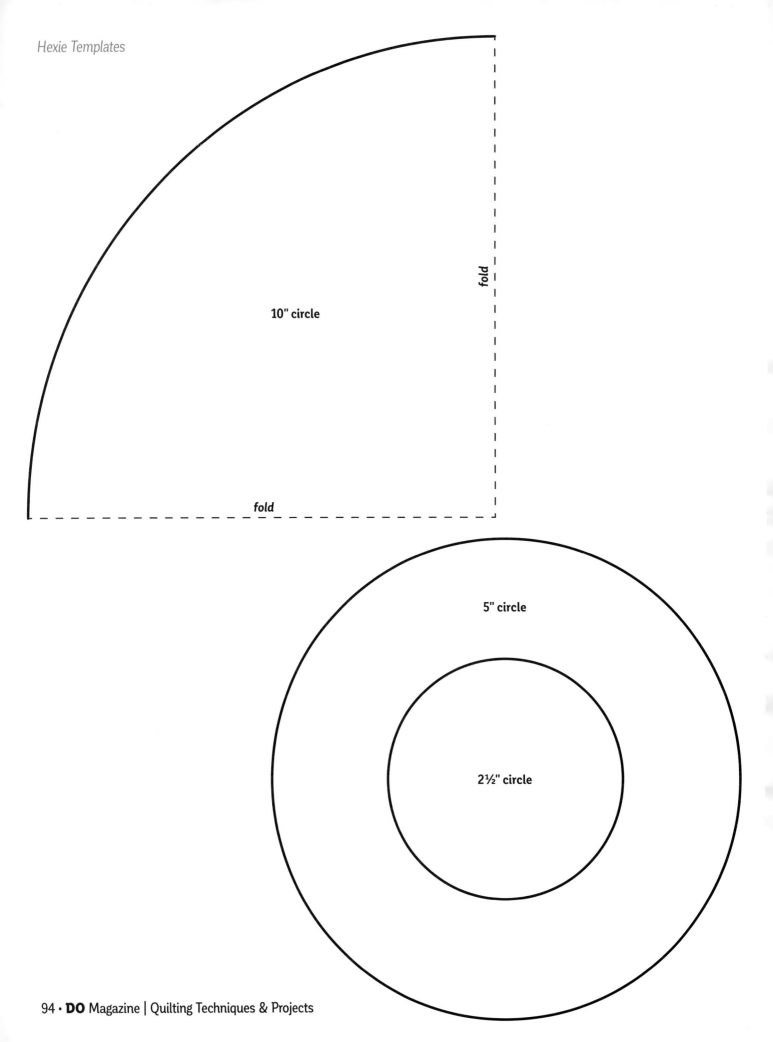

10" circle

fold

fold

5" circle

2½" circle

Contributors

✦ Patricia Sanabria-Friederich

Patricia Sanabria-Friederich is part-owner of her family quilt shop in San Joaquin De Flores, Costa Rica, where she grew up. The shop is graciously named in honor of her grandmother El Baul De Mi Abuelita which translates to "My Grandmother's Trunk." Patricia lives in Cedarburg, Wisconsin, with her husband, Doyle, and has two grown sons, all of who support and encourage her love of quilts and quilt making.

✦ Janet Houts

For Janet Houts, drawing geometric shapes and designs and turning them into quilt designs came naturally. She began her career in graphic arts, translated it to quilting and now designs quilts for several textile companies. Her quilts have been published in numerous quilting magazines. She and her husband, Steven, reside in the Sun Valley area of Idaho where she receives much inspiration from the beautiful natural surrounds. She is co-author of *Circle of Nine*, and *Log Cabin Quilts: The Basics & Beyond*.

✦ Jean Ann Wright

Jean Ann Wright can't remember a time when she didn't know how to sew. She majored in textiles and fine art, combining her love of sewing and fashion design with her love of painting and drawing. Jean Ann was editor of *Quilt Magazine* for 20 years and is now an author, a quilt designer, and a consultant to the quilting industry. Jean Ann has had quilts featured on the covers of *The Quilter* and *Quilter's World*. She is the author of *Quilting Sashings & Settings: The Basics & Beyond*, *Jelly Roll Jambalaya*, and co-author of *Circle of Nine*, *Log Cabin Quilts: The Basics & Beyond*.

✦ Wendy Sheppard

Wendy Sheppard, author of *Recreating Antique Quilts*, is originally from Southeast Asia and began her career as a chemical engineer. In 2005, with encouragement from a friend and no prior sewing experience, she made her first quilt. Needless to say, that adventure into quilting changed her career path. Wendy's original designs have been featured in numerous publications, including *The Quilter*, *Quilt Trend*, *American Patchwork & Quilting*, *Fons and Porter's Love of Quilting* and many others. She also designs patterns for Benartex, RJR Fabrics, Quilting Treasures, and Island Batiks. In addition to her design work, Wendy shares her free-hand and machine quilting designs and tips on her website (ivoryspring.wordpress.com) and blog (*Thread Talk from My Sewing Machine*). Currently she resides in northern Virginia with her family.

✦ Mary M. Hogan

Mary M. Hogan has been quilting for about 25 years and sewing since she was 9 or 10 years old. Retired from her day job, she spends both days and evenings quilting, designing, writing, and teaching. Passionate about sharing quilting with others, she teaches regularly at her local quilt shop and is available to lecture and teach wherever quilters gather.

✦ McB McManus and E.B. Updegraff

A quilting partnership started years ago when McB McManus and E.B. Updegraff met while working for Landauer Publishing. Together and separately, they have created quilts, tutorials, and projects for the fans and followers of Landauer Publishing and for their friends, family, and community. Through their friendship, they design quilts as a team: McB takes on the piecing, while E.B. does the quilting. They happily share the task of shopping for and selecting fabrics. McB and E.B both live in Des Moines, IA.

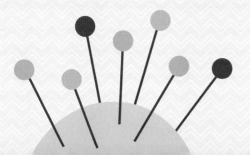

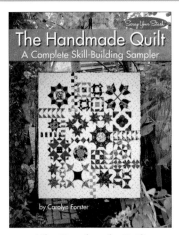
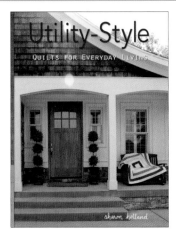

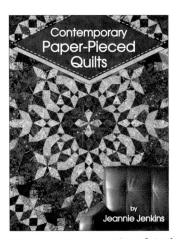